BE LOVE

A Book about Awakening

NED BURWELL

Becky,
Such a pleasure to
meet you today! It brings
me great joy to hear about
your experiences and celebrations. may you
from reading this book. fall deeply in love
continue to with yourself. You are love.

Be love.

Be Love
A Book about Awakening
By Ned Burwell

Edited By Myrna Riback

ISBN-13: 978-1719463805
ISBN-10: 1719463808

Umatter publications
1713 Richmond St
Dorchester ON
N0L 1G0 P.O. Box. 284

www.nedburwell.com

Body, Mind & Spirit, Inspiration & Personal Growth

TABLE OF CONTENTS

DEDICATION

This book is dedicated to four of my greatest teachers: my wife, Lisa Burwell, my mother, Mary Burwell, my father, Tim Burwell, and my grandmother, Anne Wilson.

My wife taught me how to be loved. Her grace and perfection has taught me a deeper meaning of love.

My mother taught me how to love. When I was a little boy, my mother filled my heart with love. I drew from it until I learned how to love myself.

My father taught me how to be brave. His creative intelligence and fearless heart taught me I can do anything.

My grandmother taught me how to listen to the love in me. She was wise beyond words.

ACKNOWLEDGEMENTS

Special thanks goes to my mother-in-law, Shirley Anderson. Shirley, your support gave me the courage to dive into my heart and go for my dream of writing a book. I'm not sure if this book would be in my hands today without your love and support.

Thank you, Sati Leamen and JoAnne Harman, for proofreading this book. You both were a gift from God for this project. You came along at just the right moment when I needed some guidance and wisdom.

Lastly, I would like to thank my editor, Myrna Riback. Thank you for all the hard work and trade knowledge you poured into this book. Your experience and wisdom were greatly appreciated.

PREFACE

This book began to take shape in my early twenties when I was just beginning to awaken to something within. I spent the first twenty years of my life covering myself. Then I spent the next twenty years shaking off the things with which I'd covered myself.

When I was a young boy, my grandmother invoked a tide of silence in me. At the height of my sadness, I needed the peace she'd revealed to me in my early adolescence. By my twenties, the voices in my head had a chokehold on me, and I reached a point where I could not move forward. My anger had come to a boil. Defeated and broken, I felt I had nowhere left to turn. In a moment of desperation, I cried out to God, "Please help." I wasn't religious or spiritual in the least, but I was desperate.

A few days later, I received a call from a local doctor who wanted to bring his nephew in for a tattoo. When he arrived with his nephew in tow, the doctor seemed out of control, as if he'd had too much caffeine. He was bouncing all over my studio and, during the tattoo session, he insisted on rubbing a homeopathic cream over his nephew's tattoo with his bare hands. I let him know that he was cross-contaminating my workspace, but my words fell on deaf ears.

His nephew's tattoo was going to take about three sessions, so before they left, we booked him in for two more sittings. He requested that I book the next session as my last sitting of the day so that I could join him and his nephew at his home for drinks. I was curious enough to agree.

After the next tattoo session, I followed the two back to the doctor's house. While the doctor and I were having a beer in his kitchen, he told his nephew to "get the room ready." I was taken aback, and questions were streaming through my mind. *What room? Ready for what? Where is the room?* But I shook off my suspicions and resolved that if I felt things were getting too strange, I would be ready.

About fifteen minutes later, the nephew reappeared, proclaiming that the room was ready; I was ushered to the living room doorway. The doctor and his nephew were both wearing a look of mischievous anticipation. "You first," the doctor said. Again, I felt things were getting a little weird, but I was just interested enough to proceed. I opened the door and was greeted by a glow of black lights. Looking down the stairwell, I could see lava lamps, hundreds of records and cds, and lots of psychedelic posters. Was the doctor a little crazy?

It turned out that the doctor was harmless, and during my time at his home that night, we got drunk and shared some good laughs. That evening the doctor talked about a lot of things I didn't understand. I had no idea what words like "duality," "androgyny," "ego," and "unity" meant. Why was he talking about the nature of my soul?

Then things got a little strange again. My host made his way across the room, leaned over me, poked me in the chest, and yelled in my face, "Are you ready to die for what you believe in?"

I pushed him away and told him I thought he was crazy. The evening ended shortly after that.

About two weeks later, alone with suicidal thoughts coursing through my mind, I could no longer stand the insanity of my mind. I decided to go for a ride on my motorcycle to clear my mind. During my ride, I saw a brick building at the end of a long strip of road. I accelerated, intending to drive into the wall at about 150 km. But as I sped closer to that brick wall, I could hear the doctor's voice echoing in my mind as I recalled some of his words and that strange experience in his home. Even though I could not consciously comprehend what he had been talking about, my soul did. His words were now screaming in my mind. Time suddenly froze as I flew toward the wall, the experience at the doctor's house flashing through my mind in slow motion. It was like I was back on his couch in the psychedelic room. Seconds later, I turned around and headed toward the doctor's house. I knew he had something I needed.

As I stood at his door, I barely had the courage to lift my arm and ring his doorbell. I was in a dark place and emotionally spent. I pushed the button, took a step back, and waited. That was the moment my life changed.

When he arrived at the door, I was in tears. He just looked at me and said, "What do you want?"

This was not the greeting I expected, and my response was, "I want what you have. I'm not happy. I don't know why I'm here or what's wrong with me. Can you help me?"

"I guess you better come in," he replied.

I followed him back down to the psychedelic room, and he talked me off the ledge. Afterwards, he opened a door to another room full of milk crates from floor to ceiling, packed full of spiritual books. We sorted through the crates and he selected twelve books. Along with the books, he gave me clear instructions. "Read the books. Then come back and we will talk about them." Then he said, "If you don't read them, consider them a gift and don't ever bother me again."

True desperation takes hold when nothing behind you looks good, nothing around you looks any better, and what lies ahead no longer has any appeal. Moments before I rang his doorbell, I was desperate. For a reason I didn't understand and that was much bigger than me, I had arrived.

This was my point of awakening. It was up to me now to decide whether I was going to take the guidance I had asked for. I didn't feel like I had any option other than to go forward. There I stood, with a handful of books and what seemed to be a faint whisper from my heart promising great things ahead.

I read the books in record time, placing sticky notes in the columns with my questions. By the time I was finished, there seemed to be more sticky notes than pages. The doctor and I became best friends, and we spent a great deal of time together over the course of an eight-year period. During our time as friends, he answered all my questions, as well as some I hadn't even known to ask. He was the answer to my prayers. He helped me save my life.

That experience was twenty years ago, and my time with the doctor was just the beginning of the adventure. Along my path, I have been blessed to meet and spend time with many great teachers, as well as a few masters.

Some of the messages you will find in this book are things that the doctor and I talked about, while other words of wisdom found between these pages come from the eight years I spent with a group of monks. Still other teachings are from my studies at the University of Western Ontario. Another portion of this book was downloaded into me—the result of a trip I took to the pyramids outside of Mexico City. I believe that all of these experiences have been given to me by the grace of God. Thomas Keating once said: "I think God sometimes picks the most unlikely candidates just to exercise his ingenuity."

It is my wish that this book turns you inward and points you toward your empowerment. I want to poke you in the chest and yell, "Are you ready to live on purpose?"

Take what you like from this book and have your own experience. After years of searching for truth and peace, I have discovered that I carry inside of me my own truth. No one has my truth but me. As for peace, it's not obtained—it is already within you. Surrender to it.

By the end of your life, you will have made thousands of mistakes. Those mistakes will be easier to live with than one single regret for not following your heart.

Ned Burwell
2017

Introduction

Awakening

Before my awakening, I felt stuck, frustrated, and angry. I bounced from one distraction to another and had a constant feeling there was more for me in this life. Even during the good, the stable times, I felt something wasn't right. I was sinking. I needed more. Usually, I sought the "more" through longer hours at work, shopping for more "stuff," and burying myself in more debt. As a result, I was only becoming unhappier in the process. I had searched for and tried many things, only to find myself right back where I had begun.

It wasn't until I started to look at the quality of my thoughts that I began to realize just how toxic my mind had become. I had an internal voice that ran a negative commentary all the time. I was hard on myself as well as everyone around me. I couldn't even live up to my own standards. No matter what was happening in the moment, I always saw the negative side. Even when there was nothing to complain about, I would seek out an unsatisfactory moment from the past or jump ahead to a future moment that had not even happened yet. I could be having the time of my life and, right in the middle of it all, I would think, "Damn! The day is almost over and tomorrow I have to go back to work in that horrible factory." I had become addicted to toxic thinking yet totally unaware of it. I had created a complex infrastructure in my mind, a maze of roads that all led to the same place—my own living hell.

As my interest in my spirituality grew, I began to realize how poisonous my thoughts had become. I began reading and absorbing new knowledge. I wanted to resurface my roads with kinder and more positive thoughts. Eventually, I had repaved almost every road in my mind; however, all the roads still led to the same place—my personal crazy town. I thought that by adding more and new beliefs, my mind would be a better place in which to live. But nothing really changed for me. Now instead of feeling low most of the time and pretending I was happy, I pretended I was happy all the time and felt like I was on a roller coaster that never stopped going up and down.

Positive thinking on its own was not enough. There are times when positive thinking is helpful, but it doesn't have the ability to deliver lasting peace. Not all circumstances are positive. Being honest and authentic is more balanced. Furthermore, being positive doesn't guarantee your awakening, nor can it expand your consciousness.

WILLINGNESS TO CHANGE

Awakening takes courage. The conscious choice to change begins with your willingness to be courageous. Still, change is not easy to employ, and there is no guarantee that it will be a permanent shift when you do. It takes a hero's heart to actively stay on the path of awakening. Your willingness to change and the courage to do so will be thrust under your nose many times. The changes required include all the habits, mindsets, and disempowering situations in your life. You will require a new inner dialogue, one that supports loving self. Along with these changes, there must be willingness to release your past and the desire to cling to old wounds. Awakening leads you to letting go, and letting go deepens your awakening. In your awakening, you don't need to know how to let go. You begin with being willing. In your willingness, the way will be revealed to you. Change is like turning a corner—you sometimes can't see the road ahead until you make the turn. By embracing willingness and courage, you enter the domain of possibility. Lastly, you don't change or awaken to become what others need or want you to be. This is a gift that you give yourself.

How to Use This Book

I needed more in life because the life I was living was not working. I wanted off the treadmill. I knew that if I was ever going to experience more in my life, something had to change. This book contains the main strategies I worked with to uncover my peace. The tools I share in the book are what I used to wake up to my heart/soul. My life now is full of enlightened moments. Every time I surrender and am courageous enough to love, my divinity enlivens the moment.

I want to share with you how I changed my life for the better and how you can successfully turn things around in your life too. But this book is not a casual read. It was written not for your mind but for your heart. My intention is to turn the reader inward to experience a personal transformation. Take what's good and leave behind what doesn't work for you. I encourage you to read this book more than once in order to discover the layers of wisdom within. You hold the keys to your awakening, and the chapters that follow will prove that to you. Some of the material in this book holds transformative power to radically shift your current state of consciousness. If you would like to deepen your experience of the material covered, you can work with the Tools at the end of each chapter.

The beginning of the book deals more with subjectivity, understanding your inner world. It then progresses into a more objective focus in the middle. This all sets you up to go deeper in the final chapters. This book ends with a strong spiritual focus, designed to bring a sense of union to your relationship with God.

This book was not produced with religion or any specific philosophy in mind. I would also like to call your attention to the fact that I repeatedly use the word God. But when I refer to God, I am not talking about religion. God is not a religious concept. God is the source of all things seen and unseen, known and unknown. God is the totality of all that IS. The entire point of awakening is to know your relationship with God. When you know who and what you are in relation to God, insignificant behaviors, mindsets, and desires fall away as you discover God's presence within you.

By changing your relationship with your thoughts, releasing yourself from the past, living in the present moment, and embracing love, you will make profound changes in your life—changes that are right, positive, and in alignment with your purpose. You will awaken. The mind can carry more weight than you can handle in your life. That weight results in a life of struggle and disease. With nothing weighing you down, you can make better life decisions, because the path ahead is clearer. When clarity of heart and mind are achieved, your divinity naturally springs forth and your path becomes illuminated with the radiance of your true self. The menial task of living is no longer your main focus. What becomes most self-evident is the virtuous path of love.

CHAPTER ONE

THE MIND

POSITIVE AFFIRMATION: *My mind is a gift that was given to me for my use. The quality of my life is determined by the choices I make ... not the thoughts in my head.*

Getting out of our thinking minds is one of our greatest challenges. All our lives we are taught to think and are praised for it. We are told what to think, how to think, and to keep on thinking. Being able to set down our mind is just as important as being able to use it. Being a great thinker does not lead us to happiness or peace. If it could, our planet would be in great shape. In my study of psychology, I have learned that scientists have discovered that our genes predispose us to multitudes of preferences. Our personal psychology, what we pick up from our family and external influences tell us how and what to think in every moment of our lives. Between our genes and our programming, the voices in our heads sometimes become an obnoxious, outspoken guest that demands all our attention.

There is, of course, a place for thinking. And we need to think. It is a valuable resource that utilizes our experiences and training. It is also equally important to be able to not think. In this three-part chapter, we will explore the difference between thoughts and thinking, how not to be affected by our thoughts, and the natural tendencies of the mind. With some simple tools, we can learn how to set our minds down.

I start this first chapter by talking about the mind. Growing up, I was soft-hearted. What would be a mild upset for some was very bothersome to me. I was sensitive, caring, and full of emotion. Later, at the height of my struggles, I was deeply lost in my thoughts and thinking. My mind had become an elaborate maze, and the walls had grown too tall to see over. My world felt like it was closing in on me. By my early twenties, I was desperate and suicidal. My crowded mind was full of fears, insecurities, and a propensity to lash out in anger.

Getting out of my troubling thoughts became a real need for me, but understanding my mind and emotions proved to be a challenging task. I learned a great deal of what I talk about in this chapter from my time with the Ishaya monks. Learning from them brought a great deal of balance to the landscape of my mind.

Chapter One contains some valuable keys to your journey toward experiencing peace and self-empowerment. By applying the tools shared in this chapter, you could experience a radical shift in consciousness. Don't be fooled by the simplistic nature of the concepts shared here. This is only the groundwork required for you to digest the deeper concepts that will come later in this book.

PART ONE: THOUGHTS AND THINKING

For years, I was at war with myself. When I decided
to set down my mind, the war was over. You can
only leave the battlefield when you begin looking
into the mind and understanding its parts.

Thoughts and thinking are two completely different things. Thoughts come into your mind. You have no control over their frequency or their quality. The easiest way to illustrate this is to ask yourself: "What is my next thought?" You cannot predict that. You can decide what you are going to think about—you can even decide how long you will think about a topic—but you have no control over what thoughts are going to come to you.

The nature of thoughts is that they may be untrue,
unreal, or even other people's thoughts.

Untrue Thoughts

Some of your thoughts may contain lies you have been told or lies you have told yourself that have become your truth. It's like telling a story in a circle of people. By the time the story gets back to you, it has changed. We do this in our minds as we rethink old stories. Sometimes our thoughts change. They can change enough that they become untrue in the process. If you tell yourself subtle lies, over time you will come to believe these lies. But we can avoid doing this by taking some time to review our thoughts before they become our beliefs. For example, when I struggled with insecurity, I had many thoughts that re-enforced my insecurities. I had thoughts running through my mind like, "Nobody likes me" or "I'll never be good enough." These thoughts were not true.

Remember, just because you think that something is a certain way, doesn't make it so.

Unreal Thoughts

The mind has a strong propensity to throw you into the past or the future. You can spend a lifetime talking to yourself about the past and the future. If what you are thinking about is not happening now, categorize it as unreal and set it down. Fears and catastrophic thinking tend to fall into this category of thoughts. Our mind can create elaborate scenarios, all of which may not be happening. The following quotation by President-elect James A. Garfield illustrates what I'm talking about.

"I remember the old man who said he had had a great many troubles in his life, but the worst of them never happened."

— *James A. Garfield*

Other People's Thoughts

A portion of your thoughts may be someone else's words that you have been replaying in your mind for years. You may not even notice that those thoughts originated from someone else's words. Once you realize this, it becomes much easier to let go of them each time they return.

I was taught by the Ishaya Monks that: *Your mind has thousands of thoughts a day and will experience 60 to 80 % of the same thoughts, day in and day out.*

You are programmed to be a good thinker, but you were not taught to let your thoughts go, or that you don't need to respond to every thought you have. You tend to grab every thought that comes to mind but, in truth, very few of your thoughts are even worth your attention.

It is a staggering fact that 60 to 80 per cent of your thoughts are thoughts you also had yesterday, as if they are stuck on repeat. Daily, you have enough thoughts to create a small novel. Let's think about that for a minute. Would you read the same novel every day of your life? That is what you do in your mind every day without even knowing it. When the same things are repeated daily, they can become an addiction over time.

The word "addiction" is usually associated with substance abuse, but addictions are not limited to just drug usage. I define addiction as a habit you can no longer control, including compulsive acts, behaviours, and thought patterns. Overthinking and replaying the same thoughts daily is an addiction, since it is a habit you no longer have control over. Anything to which you have conditioned yourself through repetition may be an addiction to you. When you no longer feel that you have a choice, you have become disempowered.

Furthermore, every thought you have creates a feeling. The body responds with a chemical process and, over time, you become dependent on the chemicals that are released during repetitive experiences. An example of this is how you feel when a friendship or a relationship comes to an end. Even if you are the one who has ended the relationship, it can still be a difficult experience. You have an awkward feeling the first time you wake up alone, and you feel deprived when not spending time with that person. Change can feel very odd, like a discomfort in your own skin. This sensation is your body craving the chemicals experienced when you were with that person.

Stopping your thoughts is impossible; however, you can change your relationship to them. Examining your thoughts and making changes in

4

your mental landscape challenges the structure of your mind. By changing one thought, you can change or challenge several supporting thoughts. This can cause you to feel uncertain or even unstable while you adjust your beliefs. During these periods of uncertainty, I encourage you to embrace loving yourself. Make time for something that feeds your soul.

PART TWO: LEARNING HOW TO NOT BE AFFECTED BY YOUR THOUGHTS

When you have been having the same thoughts for years, it can be very difficult to suddenly stop yourself from thinking in certain ways or replaying the same stories in your mind. Your closest friends or family members may be happy if you stop telling your stories but, for you, it can be very difficult. The stories in your head may never grow old, mainly because you play the lead role. However, to others, your stories may be like nails on a chalkboard.

The key is to notice your repetitive thoughts. What is occupying your mind? Are those thoughts worth keeping? The answer can be very enlightening. Taking inventory of your mind is a great practice. You may be alarmed by all your negative thoughts, but when you discover what is going on between your ears, you will recognize that you need to change your relationship with your thoughts. You will see that the contents of your mind are not only self-deprecating but also deeply disempowering.

What you think about has an impact on your consciousness and the degree to which you are empowered. Holding thoughts that are not rooted in truth only takes you away from your ability to become strong and empowered. The following chart is a useful tool in identifying which of your thoughts are empowering and which are disempowering. It can be used as a tool to bring greater awareness into your life.

HOW TO USE THE CHART

First, identify a specific issue that you want to overcome. Then locate where your issue is on the chart. Go to the top chart and embrace one of the words you find as a way to rise above your current situation.

For example: You are feeling anxious about going shopping at mall. Anxiety is located on the bottom chart. Now go to the above chart, "Empowering Emotions and Mindsets," and find a word or words you can identify with around your situation. You can replace "anxiety" and embrace your situation with "trust" or "courage" instead—or any other word located in the above section. In your mind you can say: "I trust that I will be alright during my time in the mall today" or "I have the courage to face the mall." This sets up a positive affirmation for you to empower yourself. It gives you a way out.

Thoughts and Emotions that Empower and Disempower

Respect	Contentment	Understanding
Joy	Bliss	Acceptance
Love	Courage	Willingness
Peace	Trust	Forgiveness

Emotions/Mindsets that Empower

Emotions/Mindsets that Disempower

Frustration	Fear	Anxiety
Hopeless	Guilt	Humiliation
Resentment	Anger	Regret
Shame	Grief	Boastful

Overcoming my self-defeating thoughts was liberating. My mind was swimming with judgements toward myself. I felt being overweight meant that I would never have a girlfriend and that I was worthless. I was drowning in my mind. The irony here is that I didn't have a problem finding a partner. In my youth, I was convinced that I wasn't good enough for my partners. I had a strong belief that my girlfriends were going to cheat on me. This caused me to hang on for dear life, because I felt like my options were slim to none if I became single again. Changing the dynamic in my mind created a shift for me. It wasn't easy to adapt this new outlook, but I knew it was an essential one for me to get control of.

A WAY OUT

When an unwanted thought drops into your mind, just let it be. Instead of thinking about it, just watch it. Resist the urge to talk back to it or to even feel the thought. This can be tricky. Remember, it is not the thought itself that is the problem. Allowing yourself to feel the thought is what releases the flood of chemicals in your body. When you stop yourself from thinking about or feeling a thought, you slowly change the relationship you have with that thought/feeling.

Over time, you will rewire your brain. You don't have control over what thoughts come to you, but you do have control over what you think about. Thinking is the voice in your head that is talking to the thoughts that have dropped in to visit you. Many people think the voice that is talking back to their thoughts is who they are. The voice in your head is not you. Thinking happens by choice. It can be stopped at any time you choose.

Note: For those who live with untreated chemical imbalances, this next part may be difficult or impractical. I caution you, however, do not dismiss this information to support your own disempowerment.

People will often say, "I can't stop thinking." The truth is you will not stop thinking. That is a choice you are making. Just as walking, sitting, and standing are choices, so is thinking. It is easy to claim defeat before you even try. People often use the word "can't" when they mean "won't." The truth is, though, they don't want to change or are not ready to commit to change. Allowing your brain to control your life is a complete misuse of it. You were given a brain for your use. My question is: Are you using it, or is it using you? When it comes to retraining yourself to stop thinking about your thoughts, be sure to love yourself through all your changes. You can have a radical shift in your mind; however, for most this is a gradual shift that takes place.

✳   Think of it this way. Suppose that, every time you got into your car, it decided where you were going to go. Is that car of any use to you? The same goes for your brain. You can choose where you want it to take you. You have the power to direct your mind and, in doing so, it becomes a valuable tool for you to use.

Think of your mind as a screen onto which your thoughts are projected. When your relationship with your thoughts is healthy, you don't get lost in the screen. Thoughts come and go, but when you lose a healthy balance with your thoughts, there is a tendency to grab hold of every thought that comes into your mind. Every thought sticks like glue. After days, weeks, and even years of attaching yourself to your thoughts, you can lose sight of the fact that your thoughts are separate from you. When this happens, the line of where you end and your thoughts begin gets blurred. Eventually, you begin to think that you *are* your thoughts. When you reduce yourself to a voice in your head, you significantly underestimate the depth of who you really are.

Your true self is found under the voice in your head. It is by going deeper into yourself that you discover a greater depth to your existence.

DISCOVERING WHAT WAS BENEATH MY MIND

Being an artist has given me many opportunities to be still and go deeper into myself. During these times, I experienced a quiet space inside of me. Some call it The Zone, Getting in the Gap, Silence, or The Stillness. It is all the same thing. It is a deep, meditative state that I fell into during my artistic endeavours.

As a child, I was first introduced to the silence during my visits with my grandmother. She was deaf, so her home was very quiet. While visiting her, I would just sit in silence as she often did. By doing so, I discovered that there was a comfortable, silent place inside me. These were peaceful times during my adolescence.

Then, during my early twenties, my discontent with life grew stronger, as did my growing angst toward the world. Simultaneously, I started to have deep internal experiences where time and space slipped away. Ironically, this was happening during a period when I felt the most frustrated and angry.

These moments of timelessness first started to occur while I was tattooing my clients. I started to notice the disappearance of time and space. If I stayed with the experience long enough, it transformed into moments of bliss. While tattooing, I managed to step out of my mind and rest in the presence of the moment. However, the experience would always fade away after my client left and I returned to the busyness of my mind.

These events were very jarring when they first started to happen, as they were in huge contrast to my internal experience. I was very volatile at that time and suffered from bouts of depression. I hid my depression from everyone, and it became the dark secret that lived below my anger. It was frustrating to fluctuate between these deep experiences and my anger, so in an effort to make sense of what was happening, I began to write poems about these experiences.

These blissful moments were changing me. During these brief experiences, I was no longer identifying with the thoughts in my head. I was able, for a moment, to disassociate with my thoughts, causing me to find a much truer sense of self inside of me. But at the time, I didn't have a guide to help me.

By removing the belief that the thoughts in your head are you, you create distance between you and the thoughts. From this place, it is much easier to let the thoughts go. It is not you that you are letting go of. It is just a thought that is flowing through you.

If you suddenly had no thoughts or stopped thinking, you wouldn't cease to exist; therefore, it must follow that your thoughts don't make up who you are. The dis-identification from your thoughts neutralizes the experience of your thoughts. They are now happening *in* you, not *to* you. From that place, your thoughts become more of a matter of fact, or a non-event in your experience. This opens you for a deeper experience. By letting go of what you are not, you gain access to who and what you really are.

A practice to create space between you and your thoughts is to pretend that your mind is a movie screen. Much like in a movie theatre, your thoughts are projected onto your mind. When the theatre lights come on after the show, the movie has no effect on the screen. It is completely unaffected by what was projected onto it.

When your thoughts are projected onto your mind, you don't have to be affected by them. If you remain neutral and unaffected by them, you have the power to respond to your thoughts rather than react to them. When you allow the insignificant thoughts to just bounce off you, your mind remains clear and ready to better interpret the present. It allows you to see a much bigger picture, giving you the ability to focus better because you are only concentrating on one thing, not a mind-full.

PART THREE: THE NATURE OF THE MIND

The mind tends to think in a linear fashion where everything happens in a straight line and progressive manner. It likes order and to have things unfold in an orderly manner. Life, though, does not work in a linear progression. Instead of going from A to B and B to C, it moves more like A to R to H to Q. Life is a non-sequential event that rarely fits into the context of your mind; however, your mind will reorganize what it interprets to fit into a linear progression. This helps it to make sense of things.

Once the mind reorganizes things into a linear progression, it then projects its assumptions and judgements and tries to predict what is going to happen next. But it rarely succeeds in its attempts. If people truly possessed this skill, it would make gambling much more entertaining and rewarding.

By not judging and predicting outcomes, you allow yourself to see what is really happening from one moment to the next. When you relieve your mind of this duty, you eliminate a great many of your thoughts. This helps you relax into the unfolding experience. It is a good practice to be optimistic and real with what is happening during your day. By doing so, you are less likely to fall prey to expectation. Life rarely produces what you expect. Predicting outcomes before they arise sets you up for expectation. Expectation will frequently leave you either disappointed or upset.

A Visit from a Friend

One day a friend dropped by. I was angry about something a person had said to me, so I immediately apologized for my mental state. When I told my guest I was angry, he said, "What did you expect?"

This baffled me, so I asked him what he meant.

Again he repeated, "What did you expect?" Then he said, "You're angry, right?"

"Yes," I answered

"You must have expected something to go a certain way," he replied, "and when it didn't, you became angry. Anger is unfulfilled expectation."

It felt like he took the thoughts right out of my head. Not only did his words apply to that scenario, but when I look back at most of the things that make me angry or make my blood boil, these are the grounds for my upsets. I expect something to go my way, and when it doesn't, I get mad. This incident gave me insight into how to avoid most of the upsets in my life.

The Dysfunctional Rooms in Your Mind

Your mind is made up of many rooms. What you fill your rooms with is unique to your life and your experiences. These rooms pull you in and steal all your attention. But decluttering your mind can take time, depending on how many rooms you have created and how full they have become. All the rooms below represent things that disempower you if they are out of balance.

1. The money room
It is practical to have a healthy relationship with your money room, but the money room likes to draw you in to worry about money. Still, some people will go to great lengths to feel safe in this room. When they feel that money is out of their reach, they will spend a great deal of time sitting in this room, worrying and fussing about their money or lack thereof. Other people don't worry whether they have money or if they don't have it.

2. The self-image room
For some people, the self-image room can be an elaborate room full of

things, while for others it might be just a closet. The elaborate, overcrowded room will be full of voices saying things like "You need to have a great body, nice clothes, expensive jewellery, and cars."

In this room, you will sometimes feel good and other times you will feel badly. While visiting this room, you will notice your wrinkles, lumps, and bumps. You will find little tiny hairs growing in the most unusual places, and you will find discoloured spots in unwanted spaces. It can chatter your ear off all day about your defects, things that nobody will ever notice or even care about. A nice haircut and colour and some spiffy duds might make you feel like you are the master of this room, but any mishap, like a spill on your shirt, could make you a slave to it. This room can burn up a great deal of your time and energy and drain your money room dry in the process.

3. The lemming room

There is a little monster living in this room that demands you follow all of life's protocols, like moving out, getting married, have kids, hating your life, or working at an unfulfilling job. It also requires you to conform to all the expectations of your family and friends, like keeping up with the Joneses and submitting to gender roles. To top it all off, this room has a special coating that completely blocks out the voice in your heart.

4. The sex/addiction/pleasure room

The sex/addiction/pleasure room can get you into all kinds of trouble and awkward situations. For some people, it can also cause inappropriate behaviour or steal away precious time and energy from important aspects of their lives. The efforts you will go through to satisfy the demands of this room can greatly diminish your self-empowerment. What makes you feel in control in one moment can turn around and be the thing that controls you in the next. Having this room under control can be a great asset to enjoying your relationship room.

5. The relationship room

This room is where you store all your relationship baggage, all the dysfunctional ideas and conditioning you carry from one relationship to the next. It is full of all kinds of stories about relationships and all your distorted and complex needs, most of which are not even close to being practical for a healthy relationship with another human. The skills required to having a great relationship with this room are really simple, as you learned most of the things you need to know in kindergarten. Play fair and be nice.

6. The fear room

This room can be a very cluttered space that takes up a large portion of your mind. You can collect many fears over the duration of your life; however, most of them will be illogical, because this room has the power to invoke your imagination like no other. Thoughts that are not true, real, or yours can grow into phobias or cause you to become paranoid, leaving you powerless in the process. Not only can this be the largest room in your mind, it can have a closet in all the other rooms. The fear room in one's mind can disempower the strongest person.

7. The guilt and suffering room

The guilt and suffering room is a great hall of disempowerment. This room holds all kinds of whips to punish yourself with. It also holds your most self-defeating thoughts, which will leave you feeling worthless. These two emotions will deplete your energy and, if you spend any amount of time in this room, it can greatly diminish your life force.

These are just a few of the common rooms that we all share. If you are to learn to transcend the mind, you must take power over all the different rooms living in your head.

TRANSCENDING THE MIND

The mind has an insatiable appetite for knowledge, and it wants to keep having thoughts and thinking about them without ever stopping. The only way to subdue the mind's thirst is to do the unthinkable ... STOP THINKING.

When you allow your thoughts to pass through you without giving them your attention, your relationship with the mind begins to change. You may always have thousands of thoughts a day, but, with practice, you can learn to not think about every thought that comes to you. This will be a very liberating experience for you.

WHAT'S HOLDING YOU BACK FROM TRANSCENDING YOUR MIND?

Your mind can hold things beyond the expiry date. As milk expires when left too long, so do some of the thoughts you keep. Mental house cleaning is a good practice. It sets you free from thoughts and memories that are keeping you stuck in the past. Your mind can be conditioned to be healthy or unhealthy.

Getting out of the mind may be one of the most challenging things we face; however, it offers great reward. Life is peaceful and quiet outside of your mind. The mind is the barrier to your freedom. By making the choice to set it down, you remove the barrier and set yourself free. You do this by exercising the choice to stop the dialogue in your mind. When you talk back to your thoughts, who are you talking to? Your true self resides beneath your mind, it holds the wisdom of your purpose and what to do from one moment to the next. Your life does not require a running commentary.

Don't take my word for it ... try this out for yourself and see what you experience. Remember, your mind can only perceive life, but your heart experiences it. By letting go of your mind, you are free to drop into your heart and flow with life rather than reducing your life to a voice in your head.

It is true, you can stop thinking.

TOOLS TO DEEPEN YOUR EXPERIENCE OF THIS CHAPTER

1. Take inventory of your thoughts. Start documenting all the different thoughts you have.

2. Once you have worked at this for a few days, look at what you have written and identify which thoughts are untrue, unreal, or not yours. Notice what thoughts you get caught up in. This is a great exercise for you to get to know what's happening in your mind.

3. Just watch your thoughts. Try this out for an hour or even a day. When you notice that you have started to think about the thoughts in

your head, just gently return to watching your thoughts as if they are a movie. When I refer to "watching your thoughts," I mean you don't get to talk to them or even silently think about them either.

4. Pretend that your mind is a movie screen. Everything you see and hear is being projected on you like a movie. As in the above lesson, just watch the movie, but this time, include everything happening around you.

5. Pay attention to how your mind pre-determines outcomes before they happen. This happen a lot in situations that you are most familiar with, like at work and with family. When you notice that you are doing this, be willing to stop and return to the moment. Keep working at stopping yourself from leaving what is happening in front of you. When your mind starts to pre-determine an outcome, you have left the presence of this moment.

6. Do you have things that make you angry or frustrate you on a regular basis? If so, practice removing your expectations and see if this changes your experience.

7. Take some time and make a list of the things you think might be out of date in your beliefs and thoughts.

> Parents comments - "Stupid", "mistake", "Lazy" — my ADHD strikes not know where to start. Realize sick people adding to my story of life.

Chapter Two
Beyond the Mind's Desire

"Habit, if not resisted, soon becomes necessity."

— *Saint Augustine*

Positive affirmation: *I am more than a collection of wants. My desires have no control over me.*

In this chapter, I will be talking about three types of desire: desire of the mind, hidden desire, and secret desire. Your destiny awaits beyond your desires. The way you discover your destiny is to let go of your desires and listen deeply to your heart.

Fulfilling my list of desires was the catalyst that brought depression to my doorstep. As I raced toward the completion of my list, my mind promised me happiness each time I manifested a goal. Without fail, the happiness was short-lived. My mind would insert a new desire within days, if not hours, of achieving a goal or obtaining something I wanted to own. I felt blessed that I was able to complete my list at an early age, but I needed to bottom out my list to fully understand that happiness couldn't be purchased. It created the perfect storm for me to begin my awakening.

DESIRE OF THE MIND

Having desires is not a problem. It is what you do with your desires that can be unhealthy. Wildly chasing your desires leaves you with only a greater attachment to your mind and its wants, because your desires entice you to believe you will be happy once they have been satisfied. The joy or excitement you experience is a temporary exit from your mind's regular activities. During the fulfillment of a desire, you swiftly exit the grasp that desire has over you, filling you with a sense of relief and euphoria. The trouble is that, within hours, minutes, or even seconds, your mind can creep back in with another desire that it requires to keep you satisfied. Chasing the fulfillment of desires only leaves you wanting and needing more. If your relationship with desire is out of balance, then it might be helpful for you to examine it more deeply. By looking at what you desire, you can learn a lot about yourself.

Most desires are born in the mind. They live comfortably in you, creating havoc in your life. Desire causes you to run in circles, chasing your tail. You can spend countless hours working to earn enough money and then mindlessly throw it away on an object that you don't need and don't necessarily want. As you fulfill one desire, another automatically arises. By chasing your desires, you waste precious energy and resources that could be applied more purposefully. The mind is very accustomed to want. When you give in to the wants of the mind repeatedly, over time your wants become what you think you need. You transform your simple and unnecessary wants into full-fledged habits.

Finding balance with the fulfillment of your desires helps you keep a healthy relationship with your mind. It also frees you from the grasp they can have on your life. When decisions no longer feel like a choice, your desires have crossed the threshold of what is healthy for you.

You might find much joy in fulfilling your desires when you are experiencing a low. Fulfillment of desires can feel like an exit from the prison of your mind. Your body becomes flooded with the feel-good chemicals of dopamine, oxytocin, serotonin, and endorphins that make you feel happy or satisfied. But really, you are giving up one prison for another. What you are looking for is peace. It cannot be found in these four chemicals.

During the fulfillment of your desires, something else is going on. The moment you fulfill a desire, you become desire-less, which can create a deep state of inner calm. This state of having no desire causes you to transcend the surface of your mind and takes you deeper into a place of peace. The gravity of desire pins you down, causing you to feel heavy and burdened. The sudden release of desire frees you, and the contrast creates a sense of lightness in the body.

Your peace does not come from fulfilling your desires but from surrendering your desires. Deep surrender gives you what your desires can only promise. Surrender moves you into trust. It opens a space in you that is suitable for the gift of peace to arise in. It also opens the door for the Divine to provide. Your job is to do what you can while allowing room for the Divine to move in your life. There is a great deal of unknown variables at work, most of which are handled by the greater intelligence of our Creator.

Knowing that this can happen is not enough. You must put it into practice. As you practice the act of letting go of your desires, be willing to keep surrendering until your desires no longer pull your attention.

Living without your desires is a powerful position to be in. It has the power to deliver you into the arms of peace and, ultimately, your freedom. The bondage of your desires may be more restrictive than you are aware. Often it is not until you have given up a desire that you realize the investment you had in it. I experienced this during meditation retreats. Upon arriving at the retreat, I was ready to relax and get into my meditation. After a few days, though, I began to miss my comforts of home. By giving myself the opportunity to pull away from my comforts, it became clear that my habits and desires were very restrictive.

THE REALITY OF OUR DESIRES

One of my teachers used to say: "Your mind is like a jealous lover; the more attention you give it, the more it wants."

This statement is very powerful and true. It is never a problem to want possessions or life experiences. The problem is the cost it takes to acquire or maintain what you want. Check in on your desires by asking yourself these questions: "What will the price be for the fulfilment of what I want? Does it satisfy my soul?" Are you willing to work overtime, lose touch with those you love, or pay with your health for what you desire? Is what you desire worth it?

Desire is the mind wanting its own way. It wants nothing more than to seduce you into its bottomless need.

HIDDEN DESIRE

If you google "hidden desire," you will likely find a plethora of romance novels. But what I am referring to is a desire within us that we may not even know about. It is desire that is hidden from our immediate consciousness and so may be hard to spot. We are often oblivious to this form of desire because it is something that is happening below our radar and is disguised in our motivation to do things. For many years, I was driven by my lack of self-esteem and my need for praise. I didn't feel good about myself, and this feeling fueled my desire to be praised and accepted by others until it developed into a hidden desire. I would do just about anything to feel special and worthy. I would go to great lengths to accomplish difficult things because of my need/desire to be acknowledged. I was unaware that my need for praise had become a hidden desire. It wasn't until I looked back at myself that I noticed the grip that my hidden desires had over me.

Identifying your hidden desires takes a degree of consciousness and a willingness to be honest with yourself. It is easy to justify your actions for the sake of fulfilling a hidden desire. Your mind loves repetition, so it can be comforting to maintain what you know while continuing to run on automatic pilot. Hidden desires always have a payoff you are striving for unconsciously. When a hidden desire obtains its goal, the reward centres in your brain light up and your body squeals with satisfaction as the chemicals are released.

By identifying your hidden desires, you release the control they have over you. You no longer get the hit of feel good chemicals, but the reward is that you are not unconsciously striving for a goal that you may not even require. This in turn frees you up to spend your time on more meaningful pursuits in your life.

Life can be a seamless stream of events that keep you entertained and busy while leaving you never questioning why you want the things you want. Yet spotting your hidden desires can be as simple as checking in on your motivations in acquiring what you desire. This type of reflection can be very rewarding. It will stop you from repeating patterns that do not serve you. Consciously becoming aware of your desires is the first step in moving away from your hidden desires.

Identifying Your Hidden Desires

Desire Enters Your Mind

I Want A New Home

I Want new Job

Ask yourself, "Why do I want a new home?" By asking, you may uncover what your motivation is. There's nothing wrong with wanting something, as long as you're doing it for the right and healthy reasons.

Unhealthy Reasons

Not Good Enough/Insecurity
Irrational Fear
Looking for Happiness –
Low Self-Esteem
Needing Praise
Not Content
Not Feeling Fulfilled – ?
Escaping Mind or Mood

HOW HIDDEN DESIRES AFFECT YOU

*An essential step toward your sanity is avoiding attempts
to make sense of things that don't make sense.*

Some hidden desires can pressure you to keep up with the expectation of others. There are some unwritten rules in society. One is that we should progress through the stages of life, acquiring all the possessions and experiences that are normal for our age and gender. Ask any person who does not have a partner whether they are ever asked by friends and family when they are going to get married. There is pressure by society to achieve this goal, even when it is a veiled pressure.

The unwritten rules of society demand that you must do and have all the things that everyone else is doing and having. Only then will you be regarded as successful. These pressures placed on us by society create desires that are not our own. They can cause more grief than joy.

Here is a question I've asked myself: "What do I really want in this life?" I found that it was a blessing that my desires did not conform to the standards of society.

Unresolved conflicts can be another source of hidden desires. Under the surface, you may want things to happen or happen again in your life. These desires not only remove you from the present, but they cause you to reject what is in the here and now. They create an undercurrent in you that keeps you longing for the fulfillment of your hidden desires.

For example, you may have a friend who is being abusive toward you. One day, you finally muster enough courage to stand up for yourself and kick that person out of your life. But if your hidden desire is to be a people-pleaser or to recreate a pattern that you were exposed to as a child, you might allow this person back into your life. By allowing this person back into your life, you keep your hidden desire alive and in control of your life. You could be denying the fact that this person is abusive, or you could be repeating your past out of sheer habit.

Some of the conflicts you have with people or situations may never get resolved. The resolution you could be searching for may never fit into the context of reality. By making peace with the fact that your conflict may not have the resolution you want, you take the first step toward acceptance.

This acknowledgement moves you closer to resolving your relationship with your conflicts.

Some of your hidden desires may not be positive, because you can unconsciously desire negative experiences. To counter this tendency, your willingness to embrace peace for yourself must be stronger than your need to allow your old paradigms to continue to run undetected in your life. The hidden desires that are running in you only add to your disempowerment and could very well be driving you away from experiencing peace in the process.

SECRET DESIRE

I define secret desires as the wants we hold in our mind but seldom express. We hold these desires in our thoughts, and when they don't come to pass, we often become angry, disappointed, or even hurt. What is it that can turn our wants into anger? It is the shift from wanting something to happen to expecting it to happen.

Secret desires can show up anywhere, but they manifest more often in our intimate relationships. In a past relationship, I held secret desires. I would work steadily for several days without allowing any time off for myself. Then, on my only day off, my partner would ask me to do something for her. This request would anger me because I felt it was selfish of her to ask anything of me. But all I needed to do was communicate my needs to my partner. When I learned to better express myself, this problem went away. Your partner is unable to read your mind. An open and sharing environment is a loving one.

By letting go of some of your secret desires and learning how to express your needs, you develop a greater tolerance of what is happening in the moment. The demands of your desires can create an intolerance and a need to control your life. A simplest irritation can cause great pain when you have no tolerance.

Desire is born from the ego, and it has a way of strengthening the egotistic sense of self. It enforces the "me" in your mind. When simple things in life cause you to have a temper tantrum, there exists a very strong sense of "me" and what the "me" wants. The "me" that is engaged during those moments is not the true you. When you let go of desire, you let go of the "me" that wants. You allow life to unfold naturally. The truth is that whatever is going to happen will happen, regardless of your mental position.

True surrender is the ability to allow things to be as they are without needing to change them.

Being desire-less allows the mind to rest by removing the need to control and want. This state brings a deeper sense of acceptance. When you release yourself from the bondage of your desires, it is easier for the mind to remain in the present. Desire invites the mind into the past and future because it is never content with the moment at hand. Your desires will place burdens on your life and your friendships. When you are desire-less, you remove some of the needs you may place on others. It makes for more harmonious relationships when your friends, family, and acquaintances don't feel required to keep up with your expectations.

THE HEART'S WISDOM

My mind's desire knows nothing about the destiny my heart knows to be mine.

When it comes to fulfilling your purpose, the will of your heart can be a useful voice. Hearing that voice can be difficult, and knowing which voice is speaking can be even harder to discern. The will of your mind can appear to be the will of your heart. The heart does not have a desire. This is a common error that is made in the mind. The heart knows. That is beyond desire. Your heart is a knowingness within you, a doorway into the true self. Your mind's desire tries to provide you peace.

Example: A paradigm forms in your mind that tells you that you will be happy when you get a car. But once you have the car, you immediately need something else that promises peace. When you learn to listen to the voice in your heart, you begin to discover peace inside of you. Most of your desires are your mind seeking the fulfillment of peace; however, your mind doesn't know that you cannot obtain something that already lives within you. Peace is not obtained. It is something that you surrender to within.

Joy is the heart's way of saying thank you for following it.

Identifying a Mind's Desire Versus the Knowingness of Your Heart

One of the common traits of a heart's instructions is that it is never self-serving, nor is it unloving. The knowing in your heart usually carries a positive message, one that is giving and supportive. It holds wisdom that guides you back to truth and unity. My heart always guides me to serve my community, whereas my mind's desire usually wants what is only for my ego or personal gain. The heart seeks to love and support, for it holds a higher intellect than your mind.

There are many sayings about the wisdom of the heart that supports this view. Not all old sayings bear truth, but in this case, there is merit to these timeless statements. Here are a few of my favourites:

"In prayer, it is better to have a heart without words
than it is to have words without a heart."

— *Mahatma Gandhi*

"A loving heart is the beginning of all knowledge."

— *Thomas Carlyle*

"Only do what your heart tells you."

— *Princess Diana*

"If one completes the journey to one's own heart, one
will find oneself in the heart of everyone else."

— *Thomas Keating*

One heartfelt act is more powerful than a million good intentions.

When you rest in your heart, it guides you toward your purpose. There is meaning and value to what the heart knows. The heart holds wisdom beyond your own experiences. How is this possible? It is possible because your heart can connect you with a divine wisdom which is unavailable to you otherwise. Much like how creativity can flow to and through an artist, wisdom can also flow to and through you. You can learn how to make this connection by letting go of your mind and resting in the solitude of your heart. Your mind can only perceive life, whereas your heart experiences it. You do not need to have a special talent or be a mystic or an intellect to access this divine wisdom. It is your birthright to claim this ability.

ROAD TRIP ACROSS CANADA

The heart can be a difficult travel companion because it works outside the realm of logic. My heart has placed me into the most interesting and sometimes dangerous situations. But, on the other hand, following our heart can make life a great adventure.

One of my greatest adventures started with an intuition. It came to me while I was driving down the highway at about two in the morning. I was driving to the airport and taking my partner to the Mayan Riviera in Mexico.

Out of the blue, I just had a feeling that I had to document the history of tattooing in Canada. Since tattooing is how I make my living, that seemed like a natural inclination. It was a far stretch for me personally, because I had never had any interest in doing that, but I felt like I had to follow my heart and decided that, when I returned home, I would call the most reputable tattooist in Canada to start the process.

When Paul Jeffries, owner of The Smilin' Buddha Tattoo, returned my call, I had not thought this idea through or considered any of the logistics or even how much it would cost to travel across Canada for several months. But there I was on the phone with one of the greatest tattooists in the country, and he was agreeing to have me interview him. He asked me when and I randomly picked a month from that day. By the time I hung up, I was shaking with excitement. I was going to drive across Canada and interview all the old-timers and the best of the best tattooist in the industry.

At this point in time, I have completed over 200 interviews and have driven coast to coast. During my travels, I found myself in a few interesting situations, but I will save those stories for the Canadian history of tattooing book.

I never second guess my heart and, in return, my heart never leaves me guessing as to what to do next.

Reflecting on that whole experience now, there were times when I felt there was something looking out for me, something lining up all the things in my path. I followed my heart and never let my mind get in the way. My heart guided me in and out of many situations that would have been far too complicated for my mind.

I have yet to regret any of those adventures where I simply followed my heart. Over the years, I have had the opportunity to sit and listen to many people share their life's experiences with me. I have driven coast to coast in Canada and the US and have done well over 10,000 tattoos over the last twenty-five years. During that time, I have yet to hear someone say they regretted following their heart.

I must also say that I have sometimes made the mistake of following my mind, thinking it was my heart's instructions. The easiest way to avoid that is to use common sense and simple logic. A blend of critical thinking skills and intuition utilize the heart and mind. Often, I will ask my heart questions and, usually, the answers come when I least expect them.

Following our heart's instruction gets easier when we learn how to put space between our thoughts. With practice, I feel we can all master following our hearts. There is an intelligence in us that knows more than our mind does. That is why I say that our hearts know the universe. Learning to follow and listen to our hearts can have a dramatic impact on our lives. The heart is forever willing to guide our life. To hear its instructions, we must be willing to quiet our mind.

FINDING A HEALTHY BALANCE

Let the knowingness in your heart be your greatest motivator to drive you closer to fulfilling your purpose. Learn how to listen to your heart. It can be a source of inspiration and it can give you the devotion to never give up. Integrity, respect, and good judgement should always be your guide as you learn to listen to your heart.

When you are faced with a burning desire, ask yourself: "Does the fulfillment of this desire come at a cost to me or to another person?" and "Am I willing to sacrifice what it takes to fulfill this desire?"

At this point in my life, my peace is more important to me than any desire. I do my best to be honest with myself about what serves my soul and what serves my mind's desires. My heart's instructions have landed me in the most purposeful moments in my life and have delivered me deeply into the arms of love. Whatever is born out of love goes through its own mega-evolution. It transforms itself into an evolved pursuit that is a gift from God. The will of your destiny is calling you to fulfill your purpose here, all that is required of you is to listen and follow the wisdom of your heart.

TOOLS TO DEEPEN YOUR EXPERIENCE OF THIS CHAPTER

1. Make a list of your desires. Once you have your list, ask yourself: "Are these desires healthy for me?"

2. Once you have your list of desires, can you identify a deeper desire that you are unconsciously trying to achieve?

3. What are your habits? Do your habits serve you, or are you serving your habits?

4. Where are you repeating patterns in your life? Do you attract scenarios where your payoffs get you a similar reward?

5. Can you identify any areas in which you are fulfilling the desire of another or societal expectation?

6. Do you have any unresolved conflicts within you? Do your unresolved conflicts manifest undesirable results in your life?

7. Do you have secret desires in your relationship? What things do you expect your partner to just know about you, and have they ever caused an argument? Once you identify a secret desire, share your needs more openly with your partner.

8. Practice dropping into your heart. It can be a very simple process. Just close your eyes and feel your heart expand and contract while

you breathe slowly in and out. If your mind starts to talk to you, just ignore it and listen for the solitude of your heart.

9. Can you think of any of your heart's desires? I encourage you to make a list of them and start to work toward completing your list.

Chapter Three
I Am Strong

Positive Affirmation: *I am strong. I have decided to move out of my comfort zone. I have the power to do whatever I set my heart to, even if that means asking for help from another. I am willing to keep getting back up each time I fail or fall. I cannot and will not be broken.*

In all our efforts to reach the end of our lives unscathed, we have become a bit fragile. Our shells are so thin that one fall out of the nest can cause us to break into a million pieces. One fail and it can take months or even years to put ourselves back together. The truth is, we are built to withstand great falls in our lives. Our greatest heroes have many stories of how they failed repeatedly. By having a strong will and perseverance, they were able to rise to their greatness.

This chapter is about resilience. It is about our ability to let things go and the capacity to recover quickly from our difficulties. In this chapter, I will introduce a series of different topics that empower and disempower us. Strong people have weak moments; this is natural. What is not natural is to stay in a disempowered place for too long.

The truth is that we are strong beyond our mind's conception. Being strong requires that we dedicate ourselves to not giving up. When we block all our escape routes, we have no choice but to keep moving forward. Our best may be much farther beyond what we even realize. Our true power lies in discovering that if we believe in ourselves, our dreams are a preview of our future. To reach our greatest potential, we simply apply our best efforts, day to day, moment by moment.

When I was training artists to work for me, I used to tell them to have the same enthusiasm at the end of a job as they had when they started. I have found great strength in holding this simple position of mind. Whether we give up, give in, or continue to stay strong during a difficult task or a difficult time, most often it comes down to a choice we make in our mind.

Our greatest potential is always a mile past any finish line or quitting point. Our only limitations are the ones we place upon ourselves.

Look at your goals as the minimum you think you can achieve. The idea here is to hit your goal and keep running past the finish line. Life isn't about doing the minimum for the sake of getting through. There are great rewards in going the extra mile. That is the difference between a dedicated person and a devoted one. A dedicated person will make it to their goal and do their best in the process. A devoted person will do the same but, by pouring love into what they do, they keep on going out of sheer joy when they reach their goal. Devotion adds an undeniable spark to your endeavours and bares more fruit in your life so it is easy for others to spot. For devotion is everything that dedication is—with the addition of love.

Your Goals vs Your True Potential

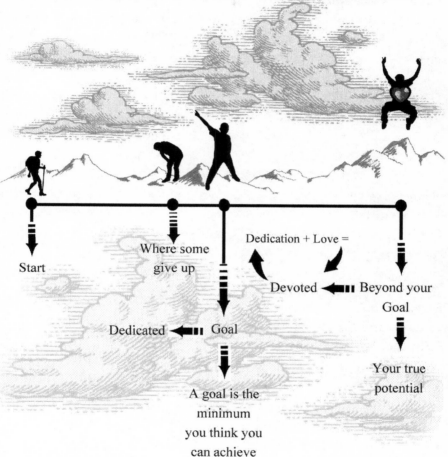

ONE MAN WHO IS VERY DEVOTED

I was very fortunate to meet and get to work with the owner of The Dutchman Tattoos in Vancouver. John, better known as "The Dutchman," was a very focused man. Along with his intense focus, he had another skill I admired greatly. He was very devoted to whatever he was doing. I found this intriguing, so during my time at The Dutchman Tattoos, I tried to stay by his side as much as I could. From my observations, he never seemed to multi-task. I'm sure he is capable of multi-tasking, but I did not see him doing it once during my visits.

John is a teacher of teachers in the tattoo world, and his skills and experience make him a master of the trade. When I would ask John a question, he would stop tattooing and explain the answer to me in detail. A few times, he even included a thumbnail sketch to complete his lesson. Then, as soon as he had answered me, he turned his focus back to his tattoo. Even when I would catch him leaving at the end of the day and flag him down with a question, he would stop and give his complete attention to me.

Since my time with him, I have tried to apply this admirable skill in my life by devoting myself to what is in front of me. It is a skill from which we could all benefit.

BUILDING RESILIENCE

Here is a great story by Abraham J. Twerski about lobsters. Lobsters are soft, fleshy creatures who live inside hard shells. They grow inside their shells until the pressure gets too much and then they seek a safe place to cast off their shell. This leaves their soft, delicate bodies exposed and vulnerable while they grow their new shell. A considerable amount of growth happens each time they do this. Still, lobsters will grow out of their shells, and when they cast them off, lobsters become vulnerable and exposed.

There will be times in your life when you are going to experience pressure. Everyone goes through difficult periods. But on the other side of these experiences, there is potential for enormous growth. Often growth is accompanied by a revelation. To receive that revelation, you need to experience fully whatever has just taken place. The struggles you encounter give you the strengths and skills you would never have known by just coasting through life. If you are struggling, just know that this can be a healthy and productive experience for your growth. It is guaranteed that, at some point in your life, you will feel exposed and vulnerable. But allowing yourself to be vulnerable does not have to be painful or traumatic. Your response to this is your choice.

Submitting and giving up does not have to be an option. When you feel vulnerable, it is usually a sign that you have yet to discover your strength in whatever is causing that vulnerability. Once you know how to face your fears and walk through your vulnerabilities, you will never have to stay stuck in your shell again. You will now have a recipe to stand strong. Pressure, struggle, and vulnerability thicken your next shell. They build your character and prepare you for the duties that lie ahead.

When you bypass the voice in your head, you get to listen to the will of your heart. The moment you begin to listen, you become the hero of your story.

But how do you walk through your vulnerabilities? To grow stronger, you will need to stop listening to the same old thoughts running through your mind. You must be willing to make choices that you know are right for you. Your mind may have you convinced that you are weak and that life is too much to handle, but each time you stand up and go for what you want, you become stronger. When you learn to bypass the voice in your head that tells you what you cannot do or are not capable of, you soar past the vulnerabilities that have stopped you in the past.

What is important is to know why you think you cannot do something. If you excuse your inability to act by telling yourself it is because of how you feel, or that you cannot, then this may be an appropriate time to bypass your thoughts or emotions. Just because something feels uncomfortable, or you think you can't, doesn't make it inaccessible.

You play the lead role in your life and nothing is impossible to a willing heart. Remember that the qualities you admire in others are a preview of your own strengths. Your greatest achievements are written into your heart as your destiny. It takes a hero's heart to let go of the voice in your head. Once you do, though, your heart can take over as your compass. If you don't feel you know how to access your heart, a good start is to quiet your mind to make clearer decisions. You can do this by taking a few deep breaths and stopping the dialogue in your mind. If there are thoughts running through your mind, just let them be. It may be a heroic act to clear your mind so the voices in your head are not screaming at you. By definition, a hero is a person who is admired for their courage, outstanding achievements, or noble qualities. That is what it takes to override your mind. Anytime you let go of your thoughts to follow your heart, you are a hero.

The will of your heart is very different from the will of your mind. Your heart understands the duties that you have agreed to in this life and is impartial. From this position of impartiality, you can commit to your life's duties with fewer interruptions from the demands of the ego.

It is important to allow yourself time to grow into the changes that happen when you are letting go of your mind. Of course your mind is useful and necessary, but you have to override the dominance and control it has over you. The mind is a tool, and much like any other tool, you set it down when you're not using it. Imagine if a carpenter held all her tools while trying to work. She wouldn't be very effective, would she? With practice, you can learn when and how to let go. A good start is by letting go of the urge to talk back to your thoughts.

EMOTIONAL RESILIENCE

Emotions were given to you for your use; however, they can begin to control you if you let them. If your emotions rule you and have become crippling, that is a good indication that you might need to work on your emotional intelligence.

Emotional Intelligence (EQ or EI) is a term created by two researchers, Peter Salavoy and John Mayer, and it was popularized by Dan Goleman in his 1996 book, *Emotional Intelligence*.

What is Emotional Intelligence? EI is defined as the ability to recognize, understand, and manage your emotions and to recognize, understand, and influence the emotions of others. Your emotions can influence your behaviour and, because it helps you read others as well, allow you to affect people positively or negatively. It also allows you grow your ability to manage your emotions.

We will be discussing emotions at length in Chapter Six, but I encourage you to read Daniel Goleman's book, *Emotional Intelligence: Why It Can Matter More Than IQ*. It is an excellent read for anyone wishing to improve their EI.

Here are five categories of questions that Daniel Goleman talks about in his book, *Emotional Intelligence: Why It Can Matter More Than IQ*. His concepts measure EI tests this way.

1. Self-Awareness

   The ability to identify what you are feeling and how you respond to your emotions as they arise. A good sense of self-awareness allows you to see yourself the way others see you.

2. Managing Emotions

   Your ability to manage powerful emotions when they arise. Having control over what you say and do during difficult situations.

3. Motivating Self

   Your ability to keep going and be a self-starter in all emotional situations. Using your emotions to your benefit.

4. Empathy

   Having the ability to accurately read other's emotions and respond to what is happening around you.

5. Social Skills

   The ability to manage your emotions in social settings. Having emotional skills that help you with team building skills as well as team participation.

It is worth noting that IQ and EI tests measure what they test for. I don't believe they are completely accurate, and results can change greatly during different periods of your life or be affected by your mood and sense of wellbeing. I highly recommend Daniel Goleman's work.

Building Social Skills

One of the things I see happening in my community today is a decline in social skills. With the excessive use of social media platforms and texting, the skills required to have meaningful, live interactions are slowly being lost. The art of extemporaneous speaking is the ability to engage in a conversation without rehearsing. It develops your ability to access and retrieve your knowledge and wisdom as well as helping develop the art of creativity. Communication is a precious gift we all share. Having this skill greatly enhances our ability to converse freely back and forth or to hold a conversation, and it helps remove awkward gaps of silence.

If you have identified that you have a problem with social interactions, the most loving thing to do for yourself is to employ a solution. It is easy to put a label on yourself and to stay engaged in a problem. It takes courage and strength to remove the label and work toward acquiring the skills or knowledge required. There are murmurs in psychology today that the mind makes up your physical reality. Diagnosis and medical conditions are real; however, they are not who and what you are. You will not get to where you want to be by claiming you cannot do or be what you dream of being.

There are many people with real mental health issues who overcome enormous obstacles and manifest their personal goals. A simple exercise is to notice where you are holding yourself to a limiting belief. Your beliefs are usually held as facts about yourself. If someone would ask you who you were, you would probably list many qualities and beliefs you hold about yourself, some of which may not be true or real. They may not even be your own conclusions. Growing social skills may challenge your beliefs and behaviours. It will also challenge you to do your best from the place you're in and to keep moving forward.

If you wanted to master the guitar, it would not be helpful to wallow in the fact that you don't know how to play. It would be obvious that you wouldn't be able to just pick up the guitar once and be a master musician. Rather, you would need to practice every day until you acquired the skills of an accomplished guitarist. Also, it would be counterproductive to beat yourself up for your lack of skill at first or when you fumbled on a chord here and there.

The same applies to mastering social skills. If you are not the type of person who initiates a conversation, allowing yourself to connect to others may be a very painful thing for you to do. If you tend to isolate yourself or find it hard to connect to other people, then this especially applies to you. Start with something that is just outside your comfort zone. Set small, attainable goals. Whatever stretches you would be a good start. Rest assured, it gets easier with time

When stepping out of your comfort zone, it is also helpful to have a few losses. Learning how to fail is just as important as winning. Some of the most successful people have the most failings in life. They have more failings because they are willing take more risks to fail. More importantly, they get back up and try again. The key is to push yourself socially. Your willingness to fail helps to build your overall resilience, not just your social resilience.

Embracing Empowerment

Part of claiming your empowerment deals with eliminating all the areas in your life in which you have become disempowered. Take some time and identify the behaviours, mindsets, or practices that are disempowering you. Everyone has issues that cause them to feel weak. Think about yours. What makes you angry? What makes you fall to pieces and crumble into tears? What silences your voice?

In a disempowered state, you may feel that your issues are just too much to handle or that you don't have the strength to move forward. If you think that your problems are too much work or that you can't address them, then you most likely won't. I have noticed in my life that when the "little me" claimed that I could not move beyond my problems, "poor me" gave up trying. Together, they happily allowed the "little, poor me" to run my life.

Eliminating what disempowers you not only makes you stronger but allows you to place your attention on what is empowering for you. A more empowered mindset looks toward hope, and hope may be the little push you require. Along with behaviours, mindsets, or practices that disempower, you may have relationships that are disempowering as well. It could be a relationship with your partner, family members or friends, co-workers, or your boss. Whatever makes you feel weak, small, or takes you away from embracing your perfection might need to be examined. You are not only better than that disempowered self, you are worth more. Embracing empowerment starts by looking at all the areas of your life where you are being disempowered. You can be what you want to be in any given moment of your life.

CHANGE DEVELOPS RESILIENCY

My ego is the part of me that complains and resists change.
It is not the real me. The made-up version of myself finds
problems with life, whereas the true self surrenders to what is.

Your willingness to allow change brings a more effortless approach to your life. Understandably, life is easier if things you like stay the same; however, change offers a great deal of opportunity to learn and grow. Change can open your mind and call you to use your critical thinking skills. In learning and growth there is a chance you will discover something greater than what you currently know.

Of course, there is also a chance that your life could be terrible if things change. When you experience change, it is important to practice patience and a willingness to accept what is. When you do, your resiliency expands greatly. Sometimes when life becomes unpleasant, it thickens your skin if you can just endure the brief storms that can arise.

The mind/ego hates change. Its very survival is rooted in you staying the same and staying stuck in your routine. But, by not allowing change, you keep yourself trapped in a time capsule. The nature of your mind is that you have thousands of thoughts a day and you will experience 60 to 80 per cent of the same thoughts day in and day out. I learned this concept from the Ishaya monks. All their teachings are oral teachings that were passed down to me during my time with them.

Change throws a wrench into day to day life. It puts you in new and sometimes vulnerable situations. Acceptance is a mindset. A choice. By employing this mindset, you can make great changes in your life. Invariably, change will create discomfort, but the experience of discomfort is temporary and often has unforeseen rewards.

FLEXIBILITY

Change calls you to be flexible. You can bend without breaking. The control freak in you does not require daily feeding. If you feed your need to control, it can become an unmanageable force that demands all your attention. Often, satisfying the mind's need to control is a fruitless endeavour that leads to frustration, because life doesn't always flow the way you think it is going to. The more rigid you are in your mind, the further removed you are from the ability to accept the conditions in your life that you can't change.

It is not that you can't make plans and have things turn out the way you want. The key is to allow flexibility to live within your plans. Being flexible helps you relax your mind. It allows for surprises. There are an infinite number of variables in how and why things happen the way they do. In their entirety, your past and future collapse into the factors of what and why things are unfolding in the present. This moment, right now, is not insignificant, nor is it just an ordinary moment. Your ideas of how or what it should be don't have the power to squeeze this moment into the narrowness of your mind's perception. What this moment should or ought to be is what is unfolding before you. It doesn't mean that you become mute or do nothing if you see an injustice. It just means you need to be flexible to allow for things to unfold within your plans. Let the greatest potential for this moment reveal itself.

Letting go of control is not an easy thing to achieve. If you find you need to micromanage your life, this may be a sign that you could benefit from some inner work. Were you abused or controlled in your life at any time? Has something traumatic happened that was out of your control? Why do you need to micromanage? These are all great questions to help you get to the bottom of why you feel the need to deeply grasp at control.

THREE STEP HEALING

Once you reach awareness, you can start to work on healing these traumatic events. Here are three steps you can apply to help healing.

1. Bring acceptance into the event that took place. Acceptance doesn't mean that another had the right to mistreat you. It just means that you are drawing a line in the sand that you're now stepping over and moving away from this trauma.

2. Stop sending anger or holding anger around the event you want to heal.

3. Close your eyes and picture yourself holding this event in love. Call

love to come and wrap itself around you. Imagine you are surrounded with love and can feel it absorbing into your body as you do this visualization.

When I was weak, I pretended to be strong.
When I became strong, I no longer pretended
to be anything other than what I am.

OWNING YOUR POWER

Being strong is a decision. Once you decide it is the way it is—it is so. By releasing what disempowers you and by affirming your decision, you begin to move toward your greatest strength. Your strengths become immeasurable. You access them with a willingness to follow your heart's commands.

Your willingness to face life's uncertainties with both feet trudging forward is simply a choice. By having the courage to stand strong, you gain the power to create the life that others only dream of living. Being second best or choosing the fastest, easiest route will no longer suffice once you claim your power. It is your choice to refuse to be powerless in your life.

The real secret to being strong is simply being who and what you are. The real you is underneath all the stories in your mind. The most powerful people in the world are the ones who truly embraced themselves. They maintain their sense of self in any situation. Being strong doesn't require you to add qualities to yourself. Rather, it means stripping away what you are not and kicking out the feeble voice in your head. The most harmful lie you can tell yourself is that you are less than perfect. You, in your most natural state, are flawless. Your maker makes no mistakes, nor would God create and release a flawed model to the world.

On your path to power, you need to release yourself from the expectations placed on you by others. Family and friends often like to hold you in the place they last left you. When you claim your power, it will mean going beyond others' expectations—and your own as well. A powerful life is one that gets us into all kinds of wonderful problems. The wonderful thing about strength is that we are always given just what we need to conquer our wildest dreams. Then, as we set our sights a bit higher, we are again given more strength. This helps us to keep moving forward.

Walt Disney was a man who was strong and brave enough to follow his heart. He said:

"If you can dream it, you can do it."

"Somehow I can't believe that there are any heights that can't be scaled by a man who knows the secrets of making dreams come true. This special secret, it seems to me, can be summarized in four Cs. They are curiosity, confidence, courage and constancy."

"The difference between winning and losing is most often not quitting."

"I resent the limitations of my own imagination."

Strong people often don't talk about their weaknesses. They are far too busy living their dreams to consider their weaknesses. Your greatest strength may not have anything to do with strength at all. It could be about having the courage to say yes to what is being offered to you. Say yes to the calling of your heart.

TOOLS TO DEEPEN YOUR EXPERIENCE OF THIS CHAPTER

1. Write down some goals that you would like to achieve. Where in your life do you feel you need to devote yourself?

2. I would like to challenge you to pour devotion into your life. Be creative here. For example: Pour your devotion into saying hi to everyone you meet and address everyone by looking them in the eyes. Another way would be to devote yourself to your work, friends, and family or to any task you are doing. As you do this lesson, allow the presence of your devotion to fill you up with what you are devoting yourself to.

3. Spend an entire day devoted to what is under your nose. If someone calls for your attention, give them 100 per cent of your focus. When you are finished with them, return 100 per cent of your focus to whatever you were doing. The ability to do that would greatly enhance

the quality of your relationships with your partner or your children, friends, and co-workers.

4. Think of a difficult situation in your life. Now look beyond the struggles, loss, or even anger you may have had and ask yourself: What did I learn from that? How did this experience cause me to grow? How has my life changed for the better? Write down your answers. Perhaps you will find you didn't learn anything, but maybe, in time, with a different perspective, your answers to these questions will offer insight.

5. What makes you feel vulnerable? Make a list of all the things that cause you to feel vulnerability. Once you have your list, start an action plan on how you are going to walk through your vulnerabilities. Note: Vulnerabilities are closely related to your fears. You can include your fears in this list and do the same exercise.

6. What disempowers you? Disempowerment is anything that makes you feel weak, causes you to fight, flight, or freeze. Include the triggers that cause you to be sad or angry. This is a big question worth spending some time on. After you have your list, ask yourself what the possible solution is for you.

7. Make a list of the changes you want to implement in your life. What needs to change? What are you not willing to change and why? In your response, be sure to look at your answers very closely. Look at it as if it were someone else's issue that needed to change. How would you advise them to deal with your problem? If you answer is based in fear, or thoughts that are not true, real, or yours, you may want to reevaluate why you're not willing to make the change.

8. Practice the Three Step Healing exercise in this chapter.

9. Here are two questions to ask yourself:

What is holding me back from following my heart? Have I curbed what I want to do by conforming to what others want or expect from me?

CHAPTER FOUR

I AM LOVE

POSITIVE AFFIRMATION: *I am love. Today I declare that I love myself. I do not require anything for this statement to be true. The most important opinion to me is what I think and feel about myself.*

This chapter is all about love. If you consistently say to yourself, "I choose love," or "I am love," your life will change radically. This simple yet profound statement can be life altering. If you desire a life of peace and love, you must first become those things in your own mind and body. And you become love when you embrace it and seek it out. By "seeking love" I mean loving self and loving others. By embracing these two ideals, a greater depth of love is revealed. The depth of love is as endless discovery. The deeper you go, the greater it gets.

We all have an unconscious drive to seek love. Love is our truest nature and it is also the nature of God. Therefore, in our unconscious search for love, we are really seeking God. When you observe two people in love, you catch a glimpse of the potency of love. Their love for each other creates an aura that radiates around them. Love is another name for God, so when two come together in love, God is present. That is what makes up the potency of the aura created by two people in love.

In Matthew 18:20, Jesus says: *"For where two or three are gathered together in My name, there am I in the midst of them"* (KJV).

CHOOSING LOVE

Choosing love is key, but making the conscious choice of love means taking responsibility. When you make the choice for love, you are telling yourself that all things except love are now up for review.

Everything you create and support from that point forward must be loving. It may take time getting used to loving yourself, but, with practice, it gets easier and, finally, automatic. Loving self is the foundation for all other love; therefore, it must come first.

An effective and helpful tool for this process is to ask yourself: "Is this choice I am making honouring my love for self?" It is always up to you to choose. The key is to keep making that choice until it becomes the only choice to make.

LOVING SELF

Love for self does not have to be earned. Love's nature is gratuitous. It comes to us freely and without reason. Nor are you ever less worthy of love. We all make mistakes, but when you do, that is the time to love yourself more. There is never a good reason to put your self-worth up for debate. You are not required to live a flawless life. Measuring perfection would require a benchmark, a previous standard to meet. Your life has no benchmark. What has come before may only be a fraction of your perfection. Why would you ever want to keep yourself enslaved to a standard from the past?

When life goes astray, that is the perfect opportunity to be gentle and kind toward yourself. Denying self-love would only drag you down, causing you to feel worse. By making the choice to love yourself in your good times, you have an easier time making the same choice during difficult or stressful periods. That is why choosing love is so important. Removing your love for self is like cutting off your air supply. Love is a vital need for a healthy and purposeful life.

MY EXPERIENCE OF LOVING SELF

The bottomless nature of love is revealed to you
when you fall in love with yourself.

For many years, I treated myself very poorly. I found it difficult to love myself. This was the deep, dark secret that I hid below my anger. I didn't feel good enough, and that caused me to believe I was worthless. I found it difficult to love myself because I didn't understand the nature of love. I couldn't give myself something I didn't have. I was unaware that we don't possess love; love possesses us.

Opening myself to love required me to be still and rest my attention inwardly. But not with my mind. With practice, I realized I was already full of love. The deeper I rested in myself, the more love I found. The act of loving myself put me in touch with my soul. I realized that love had never left me. It was I that had left the presence of love. By spending time with my soul, I also realized that when you love yourself, you are surrounded by the presence of God. Love for self not only nourishes us but enhances our relationship with the Divine.

Loving self draws love into us, and I have come to know that I can ask for love and it will come. No matter where you are or what you are doing, love is accessible. It is as close as your next breath. Applying self-love is not an action you only perform once. It is a practice that you bring into your life and eventually it becomes second nature.

CONDITIONAL LOVE

Love makes a lousy prisoner. While in custody, it will begin to dissolve and vanish from your entrapment. When you personalize love, it is reduced to a possession and its power is diminished. Love's omnipotent power is only fully present when you stake no claim to it and give it freely to the world around you.

Love is not a possession. It is a gift that is shared. But how you were taught to love doesn't always teach the true spirit of love. Children are often praised and shown love if they are good and act according to the rules. If they are useful, entertaining, or talented, they may even receive extra love. This can cause the child to have an expectation that love comes as a reward: do something nice for someone, and you get more love.

In turn, this teaching can later create problems in relationships. When you give your love to another, you may have the expectation that you will receive something in return for your generosity. When love is given for reward, or for the need of a reward, it is a love that may be conditional.

Removing the conditions from love requires a closer look at oneself. Personal traumas are one of the greatest referring factors that drive people to be conditional with love. You may have been hurt by a stranger or, worse yet, by someone you love. Where do your walls come up and make you pull back from another? If you were to make a list of reasons why you would terminate a relationship with a friend or a partner, some of the reasons on your list would correlate with your morals, and a great many would be in correlation with your traumas. Your old wounds can disempower you and cause you to retract your love.

All the conditions you place on your willingness to love will hold you back and disempower you in the process, but by releasing your traumas, your ability to love unconditionally occurs more freely.

END THE SELF-VIOLENCE

A crucial step toward loving yourself is to end self-violence. People are violent with themselves for many reasons, none of which are positive or productive. You will need to set down any dialogue in your mind or behaviour that is not respectful and kind to yourself, including overly critical self-analysis. Loving yourself means that you don't scream at yourself in your mind. If the things you say to yourself would be offensive coming from another, you need to create a healthier dialogue in your mind.

My friend, Jeff Roberts, shared this story about himself with me. Plagued by depression and suicide attempts, alone in his head and hiding from his feelings and emotions, he truly was a lost soul. At the beginning of a ninety-day program for flushing substances out of his body, surrounded by strangers who were also suffering emotional pain, he had no choice but to face his emotions head-on. He had to re-learn himself, find himself, and that was a very frightening thing to do.

One unique yet impactful exercise given to him was to write down all the negative things he had told himself throughout the day. The list was long and what he wrote was terrible and filled with many negative thoughts. "Why bother?" "I hate myself." "I hate my life." "I am a loser." Once he was finished the list, he handed it to his counsellor.

During the course of the next six weeks of group therapy and one-on-one counsel, he completely forgot about his list. Then, one sunny day while resting in a hammock, another person taking the program approached him. This person, using a negative tone, began saying unsavory things to him like: "Why are you even here?" "You're just a loser." "You're just wasting time."

After a few minutes, Jeff began to get angry and frustrated with this person and was getting ready to hit him. Jeff's counsellor intervened, stuck a piece of paper in his face and said, "If he can't say these things to you, why on earth is it okay for you to say them to yourself?"

Jeff was astounded. From that point forward, he was cautious about how and what he thought about himself. He still needed to practice some mindfulness technique like self-awareness, self-compassion, and self-love, but it was a powerful experience—one he felt everyone could benefit from.

It is easy to start being unkind to yourself, but it is much harder to stop the dialogue in your mind once it becomes a habit. It starts with snide remarks like, "That was dumb," or occasionally calling yourself an idiot, but over time, these statements can turn into, "I am dumb" or "I am an idiot." This happens when you personalize these statements. You turn them onto yourself. These remarks become possessive and, in saying them, you transmute the idea into your new-formed identity.

The longest standing battle in your life is not being fought outside of yourself; it is the one that is happening in your mind. The arguing and temper tantrums in your mind will continue until you decide that the war is over. When you decide to love yourself, your desire to wrestle with your internal conflictions loses its spark. You begin to realize that some dialogues are not worth the effort it takes to keep them alive.

The irony here is that it takes two people to have an argument. So who are you arguing with? When you notice you are getting frustrated, pause and ask yourself, "What do I require in this moment?" Often, all the moment requires is for you to take a deep breath and relax.

Self-violence is any thought, behaviour, or action that takes you away from your relationship of loving yourself, and it happens in many ways. It is not just the angry voice in your head. It is also the voice that repeats the same commentary that's trapped in your mind. When a collection of thoughts causes you stress, worry, or anxiety, it is violent to allow yourself to keep thinking those thoughts. If you notice that you're having "looping" thoughts, remember that you can choose to set them down. Tell yourself that you are choosing love, not a war in your mind. This doesn't mean that you will never subject yourself to unpleasant situations; however, if your choices don't bear fruit, be willing to make the necessary changes to support your love for self.

If the voice in your head tells you that you can't do something or that you're not good enough, don't listen. Reject that voice. It will get quieter and less obtrusive every time you don't talk back to it. Eventually, it will become only a whisper that tries to get your attention from time to time.

The love you experience corresponds to the love you have for yourself. In time, as you learn to love yourself, the world will begin to reflect that back to you. Like attracts like. If you're loving with yourself, you will draw loving people to you. If you are grumpy, you might just find yourself surrounded by lots of grumpy people. By rejecting the self-defeating commentary, you will no longer feel that you cannot do whatever you put your heart to, and you will realize that you are good enough.

Self-violence can sometimes be a habit that is created over an extended period, so working your way out may require dedication and practice. Self-violence can also be a learned behaviour from your environment. If necessary, place sticky notes around your home to remind you to be gentle and loving toward yourself.

Ending self-violence can be as simple as making the decision to be kind to the world, to other people, and to yourself. Kindness is a simple and effortless way to love yourself and others. Kindness is love in motion, for hidden inside the act of kindness is love.

LOVE VERSUS FEAR

Fear cannot live in a house love rules.

Fear is a healthy response to dangerous situations in life; however, if nothing is happening that warrants fear to arise in you, it can become a disempowering behaviour that can be detrimental to your mental health and overall wellbeing. One of the ways to access deeper levels of love is to work at reducing your fears. Fear has a way of creating the illusion that you are trapped in your current situation. It also prevents you from going after your heart's destiny.

Love yourself enough to reach for your dreams. Love gives your dreams permission to become your reality. Look for the ways fear has limited you and kept you in the safety box. Many people today pile loads of stress and anxiety on their plates because of fear. Benign sounding statements like, "Eat all your food because there are starving children in the world" are based in fear. You can't eat enough green beans to cure starvation, nor do you need to fixate on the world's problems over dinner. There are many examples of fears that get passed on from one generation to the next.

It is healthy to have logical fears, but when fear creates immobility in you or causes you to over-feed your children, you have taken it too far. Most fears are not about your present reality unfolding around you. They come when your mind takes you into a past or future moment—one you don't want to live or relive. If fear is immobilizing you, ask yourself if what you are fearful of is happening at that moment. Is your fear valid?

UNDERSTANDING FEAR

Fear is not the opposite of love. Love stands alone as a powerful force that has no opposite. Some might think that the opposite of love is hate, but this is simply not true. Hate is an emotion that we experience, but love is far greater than an emotion. We can feel love and express love, but that doesn't define the nature of love. Love is divine. God and love are inseparable, for love is to God as the weave is to cloth. Therefore, love is omnipotent. Hence, love cannot have an opposite, since that would infer that God has an opposite. Conversely, when you are fearful, it diminishes your ability to love freely. Fear weakens your spirit and dissolves your power to a finite nature. In a world of problems, make none of them your own. This doesn't mean you abandon being compassionate and caring. It means you don't let the fear of a situation disempower you.

Worry, like fear, is also a great slayer of love. Worry is born out of fear. Worry is fear taking ownership of your mind and body. Make worry an unwelcome guest in your life. Make no allowance for it to contaminate your mind and body. The problem with worry is that it has the same effect on you as fear. It lands at your feet, weighing you down, rendering you powerless. Love, on the other hand, strengthens body and mind while empowering you to accomplish the most seemingly impossible tasks. Love's reach is beyond the mind's comprehension. When you notice worry and fear taking over your mind, start a new practice of inserting love. For example, if your partner is driving home in a bad snowstorm, instead of worrying about them, say prayer and send them love. Be creative and replace your fears with courage, hope, love, acceptance, or even rational thinking. Remember, most fears involve you being a fortune teller—they have you predicting a future moment that has yet to come.

FINDING LOVE

You are like an ocean. On the surface, there may be waves and storms. However, you contain deep, still waters. May your heart be the anchor that draws you into the depths of your soul during your darkest night. For your heart always knows its way home to love, even in the fiercest of storms.

You do not need to search for love. You just return to it within yourself. Your love does not come from another. Believing that is a critical error. The nature of love is gratuitous and comes to you freely and without reason. If you ask, love will arise. Love's reach is infinite. It can find you in your darkest times just by you asking for it and being willing to receive it. Love doesn't live in a faraway place or a difficult space. It is here now. Once you find love within, you can expand it by turning your attention on it, then resting in the love found in you.

Resting in your love can be like a meditation. It can also be a wonderful way to return to a calm space when you are experiencing emotions or elevated levels of stress and anxiety. Think about a time when you were loved or when you loved a person, place, or thing. Call up that memory and feel it. Once you can feel it, now just rest in it. If other thoughts arise, just let them float away, and rest in the feeling of love.

CHARACTERISTICS OF LOVE

The more love you put into life, the more life you find in love.

A life without love is not a life at all. Love brings understanding to the most unexplainable situations because love pulls you deeper into yourself and connects you with a Divine wisdom. God is like a radio station, and love is what you tune in to in order to be connected. God is the transmitter; the Holy Spirit, the wave; and you, the receiver.

Love's silent nature embraces you and brings meaning to your endeavours. It knows perseverance. For it is there with you during your toughest times, giving you just the right support you need to push you further than you thought possible. Love fits anywhere, anytime. Love is malleable. Love's nature is simple yet impossible to describe because of the depth that it contains. Love is without limit. There is no cap on how much of it is available for you to experience and share with yourself and the world. Your life is one grand opportunity to love, and it is in Love that you find your greatest instructions for life.

When you practice unconditional love, you are less likely to judge yourself and others. This type of love allows you to see everyone from a different point of view. When you love, you find your likeness in, rather than your difference from, others. Seeing yourself in others makes you more compassionate. Learn to love yourself and the world and watch how life just gets sweeter by the day.

If there were a recipe for a rich and full life, invariably you would find that love is the first and most essential ingredient.

LOVING THE WORLD

Love is an ever-expanding presence in life that grows within you every time it is given away. This expansion enriches your life and enlivens your connection with others. Often, love is held back and reserved for a select few called family, friends, or partner. To hold back your love and to restrict it to a select few diminishes your ability to tap into a much larger aspect of love. Anytime you share your love with another there is an automatic presence of God in that moment. People often withhold their love for fear of getting hurt. This closes the door for more love to come to you. Unconditional love gives and never needs or takes. By expecting love to be returned when you give it, you are really just lending love. But when you lend something, it doesn't always return in the same condition you lent it, if it returns at all.

When developing your love for the world, it is important to understand that some people are acting in accordance with their consciousness. When they act out and project their stress or anger on you, try to remember that this is an opportunity to practice unconditional love. When people act out, it's a good indication that they are most likely in need of your love. By not taking other people's problems personally, you're able to stand back and just hold them in perfect love. When you do this, you provide a safe environment for others to rise to a greater potential within themselves.

I am reminded of a Buddhist story.

One day while Buddha was teaching, he was being harassed by a person in the crowd who kept yelling throughout his entire teaching. Someone in the crowd asked Buddha why he didn't ask the antagonist to leave? Buddha's response was: "If someone offers you a gift which you are not willing to receive, to whom does it belong?"

— Source Unknown

This Buddhist teaching has been a power tool for me. It has taught me that I don't have to take other people's gifts of anger just because they are offering it to me.

If you find it hard to practice unconditional love with strangers, start with your partner or a family member. In the moments where you are being tested by someone, try to remember they are offering a gift you are not willing to receive. It requires nothing to give your love to others. The transaction is free. Everyone can give unconditional love.

At the very least, practice with yourself. Find the most lovable aspects of yourself and share them with the world. Give every person you meet a reason to think about you later. You can accomplish this by anchoring your focus on the love that resides in you. The nature of love is wise and all knowing. By sharing your love with the world, you will begin to see more love in your life.

Without love, you are powerless. Love takes you into a direct relationship with God and delivers unending peace. The exploration of love leaves you rich in body, mind, and spirit. It evokes the power of God to dwell within your heart. The enlightened beings who have come to this earth have all radiated a love that has helped humanity evolve. By uniting the lover and the beloved within, you too radiate a Divine love that transforms the world. This union is developed when love becomes your reason and the driving force in your life. Each time you choose love, you purify and amplify your entire being. When you place nothing before your willingness to love, the result is peace.

THE THREE CHOICES TO MAKE DAILY

1. Be loving to yourself

2. Be loving to other people

3. Be loving to the world

What wonder is love? The entire universe cannot contain it yet it lives within us with full consciousness of its own magnificence.

TOOLS TO DEEPEN YOUR EXPERIENCE

1. Spend a day choosing love. If someone speaks to you, respond with love. Everything you do, hold the intention of love while you do it.

2. Take some time to review where you need to bring more love into your life. Are there any places you need to insert more love for yourself or others?

3. Are you kind to yourself? This includes how you talk to yourself in your mind. If not, practice letting go of any dialogue that is unkind.

4. Make a list of all the reasons why you would terminate a relationship with a friend or partner. Take some time to review why you feel the

way you do. Are there any wounds that you need to heal from the past?

5. Do your fears trap you or cause you to hold back your love in fear of getting hurt? If so, take whatever steps you can to let go of your fear. Bring logic around your fears and insert love wherever you can.

6. Do you worry about things that are not happening in the moment? When you notice that you're doing this, be willing to set down your worries.

7. Practice doing the meditation exercise on love. Think about a time when you were loved or when you loved a person, place, or thing. Call up that memory and feel it. Once you can feel it, now just rest in it. If other thoughts arise, just let them float away and rest in the feeling of love. It can also be helpful to slow down your breathing and hold your attention on your heart.

8. For a day, practice holding everyone you see in love. Try to see yourself in others. Find similarities in everyone you meet.

CHAPTER FIVE

AWAKENING TO THE MOMENT

POSITIVE AFFIRMATION: *Awakening to the Moment. Address This Moment with a sense of wonderment and innocence, for it is the doorway into your deepest joy.*

Life is happening in a series of moments. You move from one moment to the next, and the idea is to be aware and capture all the moments of your life. I have missed many moments in my life by being stuck in my mind. I was stuck, but life kept rolling on without me. What happened in those moments that I can't remember?

What is this moment and how does one stay present with it? This chapter addresses these very questions and then takes you deeper into concepts beyond your mind.

By missing moments of your life, you miss what life has in store for you and what you can offer the world in return. The Japanese term *ichi-go ichi-e* means "never again" or "one chance in a lifetime." It reminds us to cherish the moment, for it will never happen again in the same way.

This moment, right now, contains more than you may realize. There is a vast amount of depth and meaning hidden within this moment. If you are not paying attention, it will pass you by. On the surface, this moment may seem mundane or just like any other. Conversely, when you fully enter this moment, you can access peace, Divine presence, wisdom, and intuition. Your mind cannot conceive the extent to which you will be given love and direction. Inside, you have a road map the leads to your greatest joy and fulfilment. Being in the moment can show you what you have been oblivious to or what you have been turning a blind eye to as well. You need to be in the moment to spot all the gifts landing at your feet and to avoid foreseeable potential hazards.

Life isn't just about being positive or finding positivity. Being in the moment can help you remain calm if life starts to fall apart. A positive person is not always a realistic person. Being truly in this moment is about being honest and real with what is happening from one moment to the next.

This moment is full of all the things you require to reach your purpose. This very moment is the accumulation of all your moments put together. Also, this moment is inter-connected to a vast number of potentials and forces of nature. Whatever is happening in this moment is no accident. You have called together all the forces which have created what you are experiencing now. A victim to the world will cry out that terrible things happen to them all the time, while an empowered person will embrace this moment with acceptance and acknowledgement that this particular moment is happening *for* them, not *to* them. By being consciously aware of the moment you are in, you have a greater ability to see and experience all that is in front of you. It helps you to be more engaged with life.

IDENTIFYING HOW YOU EXIT THE MOMENT

Life is an adventure best understood by
living it one moment at a time.

When you are not in the moment, you fall out of context with what is happening around you. This also happens when you get stuck in your head, lost in your thoughts. You can lose touch with the truth.

This was something that happened to me frequently. My mind would make up a story and, before I found out if it was true or not, I would begin reacting. Jealousy is a great example of this. In my past, I would let my jealous thoughts invade my mind to the point where I would become angry at my partner. Even though I had no proof, I couldn't seem to find a way out of my delusions. In those moments, I would completely lose touch with the truth.

As you build experiences, your mind begins to catalogue, searching for similarities from your past to your current moments. Immediately upon finding a match, your mind will try to predict what is going to happen next. The problem is that you don't always see what is truly happening in the moment when you are distracted by your assumptions. Sometimes you just see what you want to see. You extract slivers of the present and twist the moment to relate to one of your past moments. In doing so, you completely miss what is unfolding in front of you and become out of context with what's at hand.

Another exit from the moment occurs when you are triggered. A trigger is something you feel, see, hear, smell, or touch in the present moment that brings up a memory of the past. Triggers can be positive, negative, or neutral. These triggers can draw you away from the moment, as you are thrown back into an experience from your past. Triggers can cause you to shut down and become locked into your mind. When this happens, you immediately withdraw from the moment.

The important message here is to remember that the next time you get triggered, you can choose to come back to the moment you're in and reinsert yourself into what's really going on in front of you. By reinserting yourself in the moment, you fall back into context with what is happening around you.

Everyone loses touch with the moment. There will be periods in your life when you find it more difficult to remain present. During times of conflict, trauma, or loss, the allure of your mind will be very tempting. Knowing what takes you out of the moment and into your mind is valuable information. As you practice staying in the moment, you develop more awareness of it. In doing so, you reduce the distractions and allow yourself to catch more of life.

Imagine you are watching a movie. You watch for one minute and then fast forward twenty minutes. If you keep doing this, by the end of the movie you would have only watched a very small fraction of it. If you only watched six to nine minutes of a ninety-minute movie, would you know what that movie was about? You most definitely wouldn't be able to extract much meaning or value from it.

This happens often in life. You catch a minute of your life and then get stuck in your mind. By doing so, you are on pause while life keeps rolling along around you. This can cause you to feel out of place and like you don't fit in. It can also make you feel as if life is moving too fast and you cannot keep up.

The mind has a strong propensity to predict and judge everything that is happening now and what needs to happen in the future. By releasing the mind of this duty, you allow yourself to become innocent, to allow what is really happening to be as it is, without your projections and expectations placed upon it. Being in the moment doesn't mean that you don't prepare for the future or make plans. It means that you don't revisit your plans more often than necessary. If you get stuck in your mind worrying about possible outcomes, you only see your past. The grace and perfection this moment offers you is best understood by living completely and deeply in the presence of this moment.

RETURN TO INNOCENCE

Innocence occurs naturally when you rest deeply in the moment and mute the inner voices. The quieter the mind, the more swiftly you fall into a state of innocence. The absolute joy of innocence is self-evident when you return to it. One of the commentaries in your mind that removes you from being innocent is the voice that says "I know" to everything. By stopping yourself from thinking you know everything, you will see the world around you in a different light. Meet the world with fresh and new eyes. You may find that things and people are not as you thought they were.

Daily I look at my partner as if I don't know her. In this practice, I see her beauty as I did the first day we met. This simple practice leaves me in a state of awe of her. Each time I look at my wife with my fresh, new eyes, I find more to learn and love about her. Since everything is in a state of change, I know she will never be the same twice. I get to learn and discover her anew every day.

Your perspective changes from one moment to the next. The appearance that things are suspended in time is temporary; even the landscape around you changes daily. Your mind likes to feel it knows everything, so change can be difficult in the mind. It needs everything in your life to remain as it is so that it can claim its worth—that it knows something. But change is a blessing, even though it may not feel like it when you are clinging to the past or a desired outcome. There is no peace in clinging to the past or future.

Take an entire day and try meeting the world with new eyes. Look at every person or place you encounter in your day like you are experiencing it for the first time. Be like a child and stop yourself from getting lost in your mind's commentary. Be free and willing to engage the world from one moment to the next. See what happens.

PROCESSING YOUR ENVIRONMENT

You process information in several ways. One is through cognition and the other is your emotional state of mind. External stimuli are processed as they enter the mind and then go through your filters.
Your filters are made up of two things: your mind and your emotions.

1.   The Mind

Many different things comprise the mind's filters:

Memories	Experiences
Education	Empirical Knowledge
Pre-disposition	Values/Ideals
Beliefs	Attitudes
Mental Illness	Cognitive Processing Style
Chemical stability	Chemical Imbalances

2.   Your Emotions

Your emotions create different moods and states of mind:

Relaxed/Tense	Calm/Excited
Alert/Fatigued	Interested
Happy/Sad	Angry
Panic	Stressed

Your mind and emotional state can have an effect on how you perceive your environment. It can distort what is present, causing you to have a perverted sense of reality. Your interpretation of what is happening around you varies with your ability to be mentally present, your level of intelligence, your cognitive abilities, and your emotional intelligence. Your ability to interpret and interact with others is enhanced by good critical thinking skills, and this is where your mind can be very useful.

With all the variables, the chance of you distorting what you see is probable. Even if one of the variables from the lists above is off, what you see is changed and altered by your perception.

Cognitive and Emotional Mind

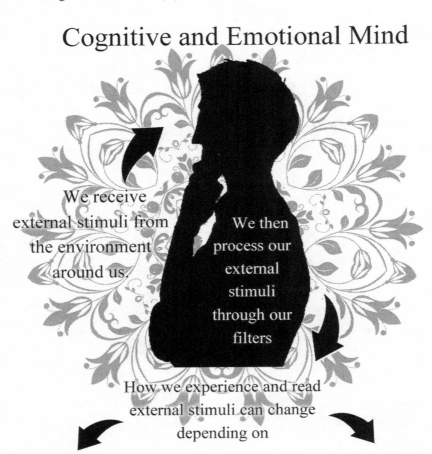

We receive external stimuli from the environment around us.

We then process our external stimuli through our filters

How we experience and read external stimuli can change depending on

Emotional State		Contents in your mind	
Happy/Sad	Relaxed/Tense	Values/Ideals	Memories
Angry	Calm/Excited	Beliefs	Experiences
Panic	Alert/Fatigued	Attitudes	Education
Stressed	Interested	Processing Style	Knowledge

Processing Your Environment through Direct Consciousness

Another mode of processing your environment is through your heart/soul. This method allows you to experience the moment as a silent witness. While witnessing, you hold a portion of your attention on the stillness found within you. This silent, still centre is where you access your true self. In this type of processing, you bypass the cognitive mind and your emotional states and take a direct path to your heart. Conventional linear processing is suspended, since now interpretation is no longer subject to the duality of the cognitive processes. Simply put, you get out of the way, and your heart experiences the moment.

Panic in the Park

One day while helping a friend sell drums at a festival in London, I heard a small child yelling for help. When I looked out from the booth, I could see the child begging people to help her mom, who was lying face down in the grass, crying and hyperventilating. But it was as if the little girl was invisible and no one could hear her cries. I quickly ran over to the girl, took her by the hand, and asked her to come and hold her mom with me. There we were, all three of us on the ground— the little girl on one side of her mom, and me on the other. I held her mom and told her she was safe and that she was going to be okay. After a few minutes, the mother's panic attack subsided and her tears gave away to a deep sense of love and peace. We all sat there just looking at each other in love and appreciation for what was present.

After what felt like an hour but was, in real time, likely fifteen to twenty minutes, we all got up, hugged, and parted ways. No words were exchanged. We did not need any. It was such an intense experience of love with two people I had never met and will most likely never meet again.

That day I listened to my heart. My mind was not necessary. My heart knew what to say and do every step of the way. The next day while I was helping my friend in the park, the little girl, accompanied by her mom, came skipping into the booth. This time she was full of joy. She presented me with a beautiful painting that her mom had made just for me. Her mom looked at me with open arms. Her only words, through her tears of joy, were thank you.

That experience transformed my heart and taught me about the power of listening to it. That day, my heart was wise beyond words and it delivered truth in action. You open the possibility for your heart/soul to speak when you silence the mind.

The soul in you has a direct connection to God, for the soul is made in the image of God. Your mind/ego is not God, but the source and origin of your soul is. Your heart/soul has no problem with outside stimuli because it *is* everything, inside and outside. If your soul is God and God is everything, then what is being perceived is *you* or a reflection of yourself. Therefore, if you are at odds with the outside world, you are at odds with yourself.

The heart's wisdom, however, is sometimes difficult to understand, for the heart offers wisdom outside of what seems rational to your mind. Only by surrendering your mind are you able to bypass rationality so that you can directly perceive the world through your heart.

But how do you get there? The wisdom the heart holds can be channeled by simply listening to it. Its knowledge is not limited to the past. It has access to all future outcomes in your probable field of trajectory and may give you knowledge that supports a later reality.

Processing Your Environment
Through Direct Consciousness

We receive
external stimuli

We bypass the
mind and go
directly to our
soul

The soul understands what is being
witnessed. It is already in union with the
source of what is created in the external.

Conventional linear processing is suspended. Interpretation
is no longer subject to the duality of the cognitive mind. Our
soul is in direct connection with the entire universe. When you
surrender your mind, a vast wisdom can be channeled.
Knowledge that supports a later reality may be given to you,
any moment you bypass the rational cognitive mind.

By allowing what this moment is offering, you enter the sacredness
of this moment and allow it to reveal itself. There are thousands of angels
lining up the moments of your life. All you need to do is stay present and
give yourself over to the moment. All that you require is on its way to you.
That is why life is truly a gift. You are blessed and gifted in every moment
of your existence.

*In between all your greatest moments, the
miracles are still happening.*

Miracles are in motion all around you. Waste no time ... there isn't a moment to spare. What if this was your last day on earth? Would you spend it sleeping, or would you seize the moment?

When you reflect on your greatest moments in life, the one thing you will notice is that you were completely surrendered to that moment. Returning and surrendering to the present starts by focusing on the here and now. You cannot be in this moment if your focus is on another one. You may find that nothing needs to change for you to be content. But no matter how perfect the moment, your mind will want more or something different. That is what the mind does but pay no attention to it. Return your focus to the present as you practice life "in the moment." Just keep being willing to set down the past, future, and all the voices in your mind. The silence in you renders great power. You can only enter this silence by staying with the moment at hand.

THE ETERNAL MOMENT NOW

*When you step into This Moment now, you exit
the temporal and enter all of eternity.*

After many years of resting in the moment, I have had experiences that my mind cannot fully grasp. I have become aware of concepts, one of which you are about to read in the following paragraphs. There are a few areas in this book where logic runs out and you must employ a bit of faith—not to accept the material, but rather to just take it in for consideration.

This very moment expands backwards and forwards into all of eternity. All that has ever been and will ever be is here and happening right now, in this very moment. You are in this place right now because this is where your consciousness lies; everything here now is suspended by your or another person's consciousness of it. It is not time or date that is holding you here. It appears to the mind that you have a start date and that you are moving along in a linear fashion, but this is not the case. Your soul is who and what you are, not the body that you are in. Your soul is eternal and timeless.

In this moment you have the potential to change not only the future but the past as well. This moment, right now, adjusts the past and future according to what is present in your consciousness. Your mind will always assemble your life and the meaning of it, starting in the past and working its way to the present.

TRADITIONAL LINEAR COGNITIVE PROCESSING

How this book came into existence.

- I met a doctor who helped me with my mental health

- I then spent time with monks

- I attended university

Because the above points start in the past and work their way into the present, all of them gave me the qualifications to write this book. This book is because of all the above.

NON-LINEAR INTUITION

How this book came into existence.

- I was given the intuition to write this book

- I met a doctor who helped me with my mental health

- You have asked for this information

All the people who have and will ever read this book created it, but the reason for it is yet to be discovered.

The points above range from the past, present, and future in no order. You don't always know why certain events in your life happen. Some of your life experiences are happening because of the future choices you will make. Your future choices adjust what is happening now in your life. This is an example of how this moment changes your past. If you have ever believed that "Everything happens for a reason," this is your answer. Hence, it explains the importance of being in this moment and flowing with life, not against it. The reason is usually just around the corner.

I was introduced to this concept by Maharishi Krishnananda. A Maharishi is an enlightened person, a sage, master, or great seer. The Maharishi and I were sitting on his porch when he looked at me and said, "Time isn't what you think it is." Then he went on to explain that the past is changeable in this moment.

I found this concept very confusing, and my teacher reassured me that it would make no sense to my mind. His only instruction was not to try to figure it out in my head. For years this concept would come to me, but I just couldn't wrap my head around it.

Several years later as a student of the University of Western Ontario, my professor stood before us and stated that, "Time is not what you think it is. What you do now can change the past."

Now he had my attention! He went on and told us about a study. Students were divided into four groups. Some were told to study only before the exam, others before and after the exam, and some only after the exam. The final group was instructed not to study at all. The students who studied before and after scored the highest and the students who studied after taking the exam scored better than the ones who didn't study at all. The results were conclusive. The students changed the results of their exams from an event that happened after the exam. This is empirical proof that the past can be altered by what you do in the future. What you do now has a much broader reach than you may realize. This concept goes against mainstream thinking; however, in theory and in practice, it proves to check out. By removing the belief that life unfolds in a linear progression, this concept is much easier to grasp.

Another way to look at this: this moment now is the past of the future. What is happening around you may only make better sense to you later. Some of the gifts that arrive in your life come because of the future choices that are yet to be made. This may be why life does not always make sense. However, there is a common belief that everything happens for a reason. The reason just might be that we have chosen what is happening around us.

There are only two things to do ... Pay attention to the moment. Then let go.

Your mind does a poor job of holding the past and future in place within your mind. It doesn't have the capacity to fully grasp what is happening right now. What you are holding is a very limited version of what is here and what has been. One thing that you can guarantee, the more awake and present you get with this moment, is that this life becomes more alive and expansive for you. Being present in this moment requires you to pay full attention to the here and now. When you do, you just might catch the sacredness of each moment before it passes you by.

Once you discover who you are, the desire to leave this moment loses its spark. For it is only in the presence of this moment that you can deeply know yourself.

TOOLS TO DEEPEN YOUR EXPERIENCE OF THIS CHAPTER

1. How dedicated can you be to the moment? Over the next few days, stay very aware of everything that is happening around you. Try to catch subtle aspects of your environment. Pay attention to where you are and what is around you.

2. Observe how much your mind fills in what it thinks is going to happen next. When you notice yourself projecting a probable outcome, stop the commentary in your mind.

3. What are some of your triggers that take you out of the moment?

4. Be aware when you place the moment on pause and get lost in your mind. Can you live for an entire day with your finger off the pause button?

5. Engage your partner, family, and friends like you have never met them. Pretend you are meeting them for the first time.

6. Practice observing your environment with your heart. Read and respond to your environment using only your heart. Listen to what

your heart has to say. In this exercise, you don't get to talk. Your job is to:

- Rest your attention in your heart and listen.

- Surrender your mind.

- Do not go into the feeling of your emotions.

Chapter Six

Relationships

Part 1: Emotional Healing and Growth through Relationships

Positive affirmation: *Love and respect is currency in relationships. The more we pour into our relationships, the more value they contain.*

If successful, our relationships can offer us some of our greatest joys and a great deal of personal growth. If we have problems in our relationships, however, they can cause our deepest pains. But our struggles with them can give us a point of focus to direct our self-reflection. In this chapter, we are going to talk about how relationships can bring up our emotions and can force us to take a deeper look at ourselves.

Three Things Relationships Have Taught Me

1. They have made me aware of what triggers my emotions. Knowing my triggers helps me know the source of my problems as well as what motivates me.

2. They have helped me know how to control my emotions and respond with gentleness.

3. They have helped me to see a connectedness between myself and others.

TRIGGERS AND PATTERNS

A trigger is something that suddenly causes you to feel an emotion or access a memory. Intimate relationships can be great instigators of triggers, but they can also create some of your deepest wounds that are difficult to heal.

Identifying your triggers and patterns can be a very liberating experience. Sometimes you may not know what triggers you; all you know is that you are angry, shut down, or even suddenly taken over with anxiety. Knowing the triggers that disempower you provides great insight into yourself. Once you can identify a trigger, you can trace back to where you have been hurt. Then, from a safe place, you can heal that experience and continue to move forward without leaving part of yourself stuck in the past.

Often there are patterns to our triggers, and these same patterns show up in each relationship we have. Think of any difficulties you have had with intimate relationships, friends and family, or in the workplace. Is there a common theme among any of them?

One of the steps to moving away from your triggers and healing your relationship with the past is to bring acceptance to the situation or trauma you are healing. Once you see a pattern, you can start the process of healing the source of it. For example, if you have been pushed away by several people, rejection may be a trigger for you. Look back to the first time you felt rejected. Did a childhood friend end their friendship with you, or did one of your siblings or parents reject you?

HOW TO IDENTIFY YOUR TRIGGERS

Your needs can sometimes be what trigger you. Here are some examples of how to identify some of your triggers. Fill in the blanks space with the appropriate word or words from the list below each sentence.

Ask yourself: "I need to be _____."

Accepted, Respected, Liked, Understood, Needed, Valued, In Control, Right, Treated Fairly, Given Attention, Comforted, Included, Challenged

Ask yourself: "I require_____."

Freedom, Quiet Time, Balance, Consistency, Order, Love, Safety, Predictability, Change.

There can be a great deal of trapped emotion around the traumatic events in your life. Acceptance may be how you start to move away from your traumatic experiences. Acceptance does not mean that the other person was right to cause you harm. It means that, even though you did not like what happened, it did happen and you have acknowledged it and decided to move forward. Acceptance marks the willingness to start moving your way out of a traumatic event from your past. It is like mentally drawing a line in the sand and then stepping over it. Everything behind the line is now your past. You now have a distinct marker to move forward from. If you are finding it hard to even make the first step to acceptance, look for what you can start to accept in the situation. Then gradually move that acceptance to cover the entire event.

For years, I was haunted by a difficult relationship from my childhood. I could not seem to make any real progress healing it, and this person would come to my mind almost daily. I despised this person for all the repeatedly awful things they did to me, but I tried for years to forgive them. Even when I thought that I had finally forgiven them, though, I really had not. Under the surface, I was still angry. I just could not seem to find my way to forgiveness.

Then one day it dawned on me. How could I forgive this person when I could not accept what they had done? By inserting acceptance into the situation, I stopped the flow of anger. This was my first step toward forgiveness. Each time I noticed my anger with the situation, I had to move back into acceptance and stop the stream of angry thoughts I was projecting.

If you struggle with someone or something, make your healing about you and only you. Never place anything in front of your peace. This means that you learn to be okay and peaceful regardless of what other people say or do. You do not require the world to be at peace for you to be surrendered to yours. If you wait for others to join you in your healing, you may never get the resolve you are looking for. Remember, your peace is not attained. You surrender to it within yourself.

SIX STEPS TO HEALING

1. Make a list of all the things that move you away from your peace. What makes you sad, angry, frustrated, et cetera?

2. Once you have your list, look for common trends or patterns.

3. Bring acceptance into what is on your list. If you find this hard to do, start with applying acceptance to a small portion of what you want to heal. It may start with the acceptance that the event happened. This does not make it right, but it helps create movement. Allow yourself to become vulnerable with yourself. Your freedom may be sitting just outside your comfort zone.

4. Once you have accepted what causes you to struggle, your willingness to let it go happens more effortlessly. Letting go can be hard if you have made the opposite choice for many years of your life. In that case, letting go may need to be something that you keep doing from one moment to the next.

5. The next step is to send love to the entire event or person. Imagine love flowing from your heart and surrounding the situation or people involved.

6. Finally, imagine that you are hugging yourself and bring back that part of you that is stuck in the past. Bring yourself from the past back with you into this present moment. Do this last step with your eyes closed to turn this tool into a healing visualization; it can be very effective.

Healing our wounds can take time and the process can stir up a lot of emotion. Do not try to force yourself to heal. It is important to go at your own pace. The key is to love yourself during the process. Every step you make is a small victory.

The Importance Of Releasing Your Trauma

The small dots below represent a small part of you that gets left behind in your traumas.

Sometimes you leave small parts of yourself behind while other times you lose big parts. Traumatic events such as loss of a child or divorce can trigger you to lose bigger parts of yourself

By time you get to this point there is more of you stuck in your past then what is moving forward.

Each arrow going up represents a trauma you experience.

Each dot on this line represents you.

If you don't heal from your traumas you leave a small fragment of yourself behind as you move forward in your life.

Eventually there is very little of you moving forward in your life. You are trapped in your past, stuck in your traumas.

At this point your traumas turn into dramas.

If you have not healed from your traumas they can dominate your life. Robbing you of your peace.

REGULATING EMOTIONS

Understanding your emotions and learning how to master them is one of the greatest gifts you can give yourself and the people in all your relationships. When you overreact, responding to your emotions can be very tiring for the person on the receiving end. Who really enjoys adult temper tantrums? Conversely, if you underreact and have no emotions, this can be problematic as well.

There are many situations that call for a response. When your partner has exciting news to share, they want you to be happy for and with them. If they are going through a difficult time, a compassionate approach from you would be important. Either way, your emotions are an important part of communicating with your partner. Proper communication helps you support your partner's emotional needs.

Emotional intelligence (EI) is the capability of individuals to recognize their own and other people's emotions. It allows them to discern between different feelings and label them appropriately. We use emotional information to guide thinking and behaviour and manage and/or adjust emotions to adapt environments or achieve goals.

Emotional Intelligence plays a huge role in your ability to regulate emotions and respond in an appropriate manner. Being able to flow between the banks of high and low emotions gives you power over stressful events in your life. For example, your emotional response to having a flat tire while you are driving to work is entirely up to you. One person will perceive and respond with no emotion, while another person could respond by getting angry. They could even stay angry all day, causing undue drama to other situations. You are solely responsible for how you react to life. By not allowing your emotions to control you and owning your reactions, you create a healthier balance in your emotions.

You can let go of emotions in the same way you learned how to let go of your thoughts. Much like your thoughts, emotions may not be real, true, or yours. You could be misreading what you feel at times or you could be feeling someone else's emotions. It is not mandatory to react to every feeling that arises in you. Just because you feel something does not mean you are required to be a slave to that feeling. By learning to pay attention to your feelings, you can choose how you respond to them. Each time you watch a feeling and stop yourself from feeling it, you change your relationship to it. By just watching feelings come and then fade away, you burn up the energy they contain. Be patient and willing to keep applying this technique each time you notice your emotions taking over. It is important not to give up on the process. The mind has a way of creeping in to smear negativity on things.

When an emotion arises that you are trying to let go of, be sure to let go of the self-talk around it. You only strengthen your emotions when you immediately begin to talk to yourself about them as they arise.

LABELLING EMOTIONS

One day I woke up feeling angry. I was not sure why nor did I have a reason to feel that way. My anger persisted all morning and then, while I was driving to work, I decided to share with my wife what I was feeling. I told her I did not know what was wrong with me, but I just felt all this anger inside. When I told her about this, a story came to mind about an old friend of mine:

As a young boy, my friend was diagnosed with an anxiety disorder and was told he would never be able to get rid of it and would need to be on medication for the rest of his life. Halfway through a six-month meditation retreat, he ran out of his anxiety medication. He knew this was going to happen, but he hoped that, by that point, he would be better and would not need his medication. But in the middle of one of his days, he suddenly felt his anxiety come on and started to have a panic attack. He knew what was happening, so he went straight to his teacher and demanded that he be brought into town to see a doctor to refill his prescription.

His teacher asked if he would sit with him for a few minutes before they left for town, but my friend's anxiety was getting worse and he insisted that it was an emergency and that he had to go right away. Again his teacher asked him to do an exercise before they left. Reluctantly, to appease his teacher, my friend agreed so that he could get going. His teacher asked him to remove the label from what he was feeling. Then the teacher asked him to put all his attention onto what he was experiencing in that moment, without any labels or judgements. He told my friend to just be a silent witness to what he was experiencing.

After a few minutes, the teacher asked my friend if he was sure what he was feeling was anxiety. In total shock and amazement, my friend suddenly began to cry. He realized that he was not feeling anxiety at all. What he was feeling was intense joy and bliss. All his life he had been told that what he was feeling was anxiety and it was a bad thing. Without ever knowing the difference, he continued to believe his diagnosis until that day when his teacher stopped him, brought him into the present moment, and removed the label from his feelings.

On my drive to work that day, when I was feeling so angry and remembered this story about my friend, I decided to let go of the label that I placed on my feelings. I told my wife I was going to change the label to a neutral one. Instead of saying I was angry, I said I was feeling a lot of energy in me. As soon as I removed the label of anger, I noticed I instantly felt different. I had been struggling all morning with the feeling of anger and frustration and, within five minutes of removing the label, it was gone.

LAYERS OF EMOTION

Often, emotions are layered. What you initially feel may not be the entire truth. Your first emotion may be a partial truth, but when you look a bit closer, you discover a deeper and more honest feeling that offers greater insight into what you are really feeling. Like your thoughts, you sometimes get told what to feel about situations. If you are angry, you may be told to calm down right away. In other situations that upset you, you may be directed to stop crying. Just because someone else does not feel the way you do, that does not mean that you are not justified in having your own feelings.

In my past, I can only recall two emotions: I was either happy or mad. During my trip from childhood to adulthood, I blocked out most of my feelings between happiness and anger. There were several contributing factors for this. I was a guy and there are gender roles to follow. Men do not cry and we are taught to be strong no matter what. This is not true. Being able to access your emotions is a valuable tool. Your emotions help you read people and situations in order to respond appropriately. They also can point to what you need to heal in yourself. If you are holding trauma from your past, your emotions will be your first indicator. By looking at what is hiding beneath the layers of your emotions, you can get to the bottom of why you feel the way you do. This, in turn, will help you become more empowered and less controlled by your emotions.

This type of work is only necessary until you bring your emotions into a healthy balance. Once this is achieved, it need only be a tool you use from time to time. Take some time and dissect your layers of emotion.

Make a list of some of your strong emotions. Now look at each one and ask yourself: "Is this emotion true? Do I really feel this way?"

You can also apply this in the moment when you have a strong emotion rise up for you. Doing this will help you learn more about yourself. Once you have this information, you will be better equipped to avoid being trapped by the same emotion in the future.

Layers Of Emotions

What is on the top of your mind can be what you end up expressing.

Screaming

Anger
Frustration
Annoyed
Sad

Hurt

Hurt is what you may be truly feeling underneath all your emotions.

THE DANGER OF EMOTIONS

When your emotions get too far out of balance, you may experience an emotional hijacking. This occurs when your limbic area (the area of the brain that regulates emotions) goes into overdrive. This causes restricted access to logical cognitive faculties. According to Daniel Goleman in his book, *Emotional Intelligence: Why It Can Matter More Than IQ,* during an emotional hijacking, your amygdala, which is in the limbic area of your brain, shuts down your frontal cortices. (Knowing this when you begin to feel overwhelmed by your emotions helps you tell yourself that it's important to breathe and refrain from speaking. Once you have calmed down, you can then respond to the situation with greater ease and logic. This simple and practical advice can be a valuable tool when you feel a temper tantrum coming on inside your mind. Just know in that moment during an emotional hijacking that your logical cognitive resources are cut off and you may regret your words or actions.)

In my past I was quick to anger and slow to cool. I found it challenging to strike a balance. People close to me found it hard to talk with me because if I did not like what I was hearing, I would become very defensive and angry. Learning how to listen without falling into my emotions was a massive obstacle for me to overcome. Over time, though, I learned how to soften my approach in relationships. Finding equilibrium happened for me when I became genuine, loving, respectful, and caring for myself and then others. The difference was that I became willing to come from truth rather than passivity or anger.

Because relationships evoke some of your deepest emotions, ranging from extremely positive to the extremely negative, they will continue to be great teachers with your emotional self. If your emotions rule your life, your relationships tend to feel the brunt of this unbalance. Once you master your emotions by rising above them, you can move into a different domain of relationships—one where you now have clarity to rise above your wounds and not to fall prey to other people's traumas.

WHAT ARE RELATIONSHIPS ABOUT?

Relationships are about engagement. An authentic engagement requires that you respond in diverse ways. How you engage with the world and others can tell you a lot about yourself. They call for you to express yourself and to listen to others. In a successful relationship, both people are authentic and real. You are willing to openly share what you feel, see, and hear, and you must be open to a willingness to receive the same.

From the emotional aspect of relationships, they have the potential to show your strengths and weaknesses, so they can serve as a self-mastery tool. Take some time to look at your relationships. Are you a leader amongst your friends, or do you prefer to support and follow along? What type of friends or partners do you attract? Look at their strengths and weaknesses. You might find similarities in yourself.

Use your relationships to become a better communicator. Openly share with your family, friends, and partner. If you are feeling frustrated, try to gather more information. This will lead to more harmonious relationships. Since assumptions can create deep struggles in your relationships, effective communication dispels a great many assumptions. Be quick to notice if your mind is making up stories. Before you get mad or frustrated with your partner or friends, find out if your thoughts are valid.

Use what you learn from your relationships with others to build a more loving relationship with yourself, for the relationship you are having with yourself is one you have to spend a great deal of time with. It is just as important to be kind and loving with yourself as you are with others, and by doing so you then can drop a little deeper into relationships. Beyond your struggles in relations with others there lies a deeper truth, one that moves you into empowerment. This deeper truth is that at the heart of your struggles with another, you find yourself looking back. Many of your struggles with other people are really a problem you have with yourself. Take some time to reflect on where you can find yourself in the issues you are having with another.

FINDING UNITY IN YOUR RELATIONSHIPS

When you clear away your wounds, the spirit of unity between you and another is more likely to be discovered. When you see that oneness in another, you then discover the greater purpose of relationships. When two people can gaze into each other's eyes and speak to one another's souls instead of banging their egos together, they are able to catch a glimpse of the unity between them. There is no longer a need to struggle back and forth, projecting traumas and dramas onto each other.

Joining together with another can serve a much greater purpose when both individuals have cleared themselves of their desire to play ego tug of war. We can join our energies to collectively seam together our potential power as one entity. Our human potential is amplified exponentially by joining together as one.

Unity is already in place and completely intact. It is not something that you need to create. It's something you embrace. All you need to do to experience it is love others, the world, and yourself. Begin to look for your similarities in another because, by doing so, you just might discover the spirit of unity. Even if you are the only person in your community who is coming from a place of love and willingness to spark unity with others, you make a difference. You open the door for more meaningful relationships to unfold in your life. You not only affect your life, but you affect every person you meet.

TOOLS TO DEEPEN YOUR EXPERIENCE OF THIS CHAPTER

1. Make a list of all the things that move you away from your peace. What makes you sad, angry, frustrated, et cetera? Once you have your list, look for common trends.

2. Trace the origin of your triggers. When was the first time you were triggered? Try to trace it back as far as you can go.

3. Work with the six steps to healing. Steps 3, 4, and 5 may take a bit of time and effort on your part. Take as much time as you need to work with the steps.

4. How are you at communicating with your partner? One thing you could do is ask your partner how they rate your communication skills. Be open to their response if you ask. This exercise could open up a very useful dialogue for your relationship

5. Be aware when your emotions arise and practice letting go of the feeling of your emotions.

6. Take some time to look at all the relationships you have. Are there any similarities among them all?

CHAPTER SEVEN
RELATIONSHIPS

PART 2: CULTIVATING A DEEPER RELATIONSHIP

POSITIVE AFFIRMATION: *Love is currency in relationships. The more love we pour into them, the more value they contain.*

Relationships are an integral aspect of life. Since the way we interact with people is what creates relationships, the harmony and peace we have or don't have shape the kind of relationships we cultivate. By applying love, care, and respect to our relationships, we allow a deeper exchange to take place. Life is more harmonious when we have peace within our relationships. Once we find that peace in our life, we can discover a deeper meaning in relationships. We can create a sacred relationship with our partners.

In this chapter, I will be using my own relationship with my wife to illustrate how we find deeper and more harmonious ways of building a relationship based on love, respect, and dedication—not only with others, but with our own individual growth.

Having said that, I must affirm that love for self is paramount, because if I do not love myself, I am a loss to my partner. When I do not take care of myself, I become irritable. I lose compassion, sensibility, and appreciation for the goodness around me. Love for self not only enhances ourselves but helps us build better relations with others, because we cannot give what we do not have. In order to have a deeper and more sacred relationship with another, we must love ourselves.

LEARNING HOW TO LOVE

In my relationship with my wife, I have taken the time to learn how she needs to be loved. In my past relationships, my love was selfish. I loved my partners the way I wanted and needed to be loved. By doing this, I was not meeting my partner's needs but would get frustrated thinking I was doing an excellent job of being their partner. In a deeper relationship, it is important not only to love your partner the way they need it, but to love unconditionally.

Unconditional love has more depth and potency to it. It entails never withholding love from your partner but instead loving with no expectation, without complaint or need of anything in return. Sometimes, though, the hardest moments to love your partner are when they need it the most. If your partner upsets you or is upset themselves, this can give you the perfect opportunity to love them more. It is exactly when they need your patience, compassion, and understanding. By giving them love at that moment, you are giving your love when it is needed the most.

Make it a priority to let you partner know they never have to earn your love or qualify for it. Your job is to hold your partner in love. By maintaining love for your partner in difficult times, you help dissolve problems swiftly when they arise. Never hold back from giving to each other's needs, even though some days you may only have 20 per cent to give, while other days you will have 100 per cent. There is no need to keep score or complain when your partner cannot give to you. Just do the best you can for each other.

Giving: What You Love Versus How Your Partner Needs To Be Loved

BEING IN THE MOMENT WITH YOUR PARTNER

When I first met my wife, I felt a sense of wonder in her presence, and that wonder has never left me. It has never left because I make it a daily practice to get to know my partner. I do not assume I know her. I look at my wife as if I have never laid eyes on her before. This allows me to see her more clearly. I not only see her beauty more clearly, but I learn more about her in the process. From one moment to the next, we are anew. I myself learn and grow every day, so I look to see how my partner has done the same. By looking at my partner with fresh eyes daily, I have found that I do not place false labels on her. It is all too easy to place a label on your partner and hold them to it long after they have outgrown it. This is not only non-productive to your relationship but can be a very dis-empowering practice to project onto your partner. Hold your partner to their highest good. This will bring you into the moment with your significant other.

GETTING TO KNOW EACH OTHER

My wife and I communicate everything, and there is nothing we hide from one another. I do not read her email or Facebook, but if I wanted or needed to, I know I could. We have our own lives but within those lives nothing is too private for each other. We look for ways to improve our communication with one another. For example, we try to see things from each other's point of view. It is all too easy to just see your own perspective. By putting in the time communicating, we have saved ourselves hours of frustration.

One of the most loving things we have done for each other has been planning for the difficult times in our relationship. We worked out in advance how we would handle different types of situations. We put in the time to make agreements on how we would problem solve our differences. We do this during our good times so that we don't have to try and figure that out while dealing with a difficult situation.

We have learned how to have fun with each other in just about any situation. We both know that if we get too serious, we risk not being able to enjoy our time together. When we stop having fun and start getting frustrated with one another, we never hesitate to say sorry and return back to the love we have for each other. In my past relationships, I would become cold and silent to try to get my point across. That was not helpful for my partner, and it was only torture for me because I had to stay mad for days—something that is very taxing on our nervous system. The silent treatment was counterproductive to my relationships. It makes about as much sense as swallowing a handful of thumb tacks to relieve a sore throat. In my relationship with my wife, if either one of us gets frustrated, we voice our feelings as soon as we are able.

We have to find the courage to voice what we feel inside. I have learned to be genuine and honest with my wife. Vulnerability lives very comfortably in a deeper relationship. Being able to express what we are feeling with each other comes as a huge relief to both of us, and I no longer need to hold back my thoughts and feelings from the most important person to me.

No matter what we are going through, we have learned to share it with each other. Along with being genuine with my wife, I no longer keep secret desires—those wants we have that we seldom express. In my past relationships, I would wait, wishing and hoping for my partner to read my mind, only to be let down or feel angry later when it did not happen. We have learned to just ask for what we need.

In my relationship with my wife, we make time for intimacy. We never allow the time we need for intimacy to take a back seat to the busyness of our lives. Talking, touching, holding, and lovemaking are important to our relationship. We are committed and faithful to each other. Early in our relationship we made a commitment to eliminate anything from our lives that threatened to diminish the connection we share.

On our wedding night, my beautiful wife sat me down and presented me with a tiny box. Inside I found a solid, silver heart. I knew what my wife was offering me even before we exchanged any words. The heart I was holding was the most exquisite heart I had ever laid eyes on. I told her how I felt about her beautiful heart and then closed the box and handed it back to her. I explained to my wife that I would never take such a precious thing from her. I asked her if she would let me look at it every day and she said I was most welcome to do that. That was enough for me. I did not need her heart, because I have found my own.

I have learned that we do not give our heart away. We just share it with the world. If you give your heart to another, they might just take it. If they haven't found their own heart, they won't know how to take care of yours. Nobody needs two hearts, so keep yours and share it with the world. But don't allow another to take it from you. They might just break it.

HOLDING YOUR PARTNER IN PERFECTION

I never look for my partner's weaknesses or faults. It is not that I turn a blind eye to things, it is that my focus is on what is great about her. I see my wife's best qualities, and I always support her greatness. In our relationship, we hold each other in perfection. Not that we will be perfect, but because it offers the highest respect for each other. We never lose sight of the relationship we have created together for it is sacred. It became sacred the moment we held each other in unconditional love. By revering our bond as sacred, we are protectors of this union.

I try to inspire her to do her best, and I accept whatever that is. I always assume she has the best intentions for us and for herself. I never hold ideas that she is not good enough or tell her what to do. I know that she was given her own mind at birth. I'm not my wife's therapist nor do I feel there is anything that needs to be fixed about her. I see her as perfect, and nothing less than that.

Your partner's perfection will shine the brightest when you hold your partner in their highest light.

Wanting the best for your partner is a wonderful way to love them, and it is always worth protecting your partner's honour. Let me illustrate this concept with a story my friend once told me.

My friend was a repair man working for Sears. When he arrived at his customer's home one day, the little old lady who answered the door directed him to her basement and pointed at the washer, which had been disassembled into a thousand pieces. He told her that it would take a bit of work to reassemble the washer, and she reassured him to go ahead and do what he needed to do to fix the unit. After a couple of hours, he reported to her that the problem was just a burned-out wire. She looked at him and asked, "Is there a part that is relatively cheap that generally causes problems in washers?" Confused, he answered "Yes, there are some hidden fuses that sometimes go."

She then told him to write what he had told her on the bill and she would pay for it. When he asked her why she wanted to do that, she replied, "My husband worked over two hours on that washer last night. I don't want him to feel badly that he couldn't fix it."

My wife's well-being is much more important to me than my need to make her feel less than perfect or to ever belittle her. This is one of the lessons my wife has taught me during our relationship. Here are a few more.

1. Kiss your partner goodnight and ask them to share with you their favourite part of their day.

2. Share the loads of work together and then you can rest together.

3. If you are grumpy in the mornings, do not inflict your bad mood on your partner.

4. You can play pranks on your friends, but not your significant other. Do not tease, harass, or torment your partner.

5. Never, ever talk badly about your partner to anyone.

6. Do not give flowers as an apology. Flowers are for a loving gesture, not to say sorry.

SACRED RELATIONSHIPS

Sacred relationships take you deeper into the purpose of relationships and are built on unconditional love, respect, trust, and the inclusion of devotion to one another. In your devotion to another, it is important to never lose sight of yourself. A sacred relationship is a relationship that is based on deepening your bond with each other, yourself, and God. There is a devotion to assist and guide each other in the fulfillment of each other's purpose. You must never lose sight of the love that is created with each other. When one of you is not at their finest, the other does their best to stay anchored in love and support for the other.

There is an old saying: "Relationships are give and take." In a sacred relationship, this is not the case. Sacred relationships are about giving and taking nothing. You never ask things of the other that they cannot give. If you are honest with yourself, you will know that when you ask for something of your partner and they say no, it is because they cannot do so at the moment or at all. You will not confuse this inability with their not wanting to do it or not caring enough about you to do what you ask.

A sacred relationship does not mean you become subservient to each other. It just means that you always do the best you can for each other. In an "all give" relationship, you don't have to fight for your needs, because your partner will do that for you. You become attentive to each other and respond to what the other needs.

These tenets are the basis of my relationship with my wife. As a result of our commitment to them, there is never-ending peace between us. My wife has never kicked me when I have been down. She always holds me in perfect love. We appreciate the love we share and always look for ways to give more to each other. Our sacred relationship is easy in comparison to the relationships I had in the past. It was not that I had bad partners ... I just was not ready to step into a sacred relationship. My ego had too much control over me.

It takes two committed people to engage in a sacred relationship. We are designed to be in relationships with others and are meant to embrace relationships with reverence and love. If we are combative and resistant, we miss out on a great deal of growth that relationships offer.

When you look deep enough into another, you will find yourself looking back.

TOOLS TO DEEPEN YOUR EXPERIENCE OF THIS CHAPTER

1. Take some time to communicate with your partner. Share details of your life or how you feel about the person you are with.

2. Understand your needs and share them with your partner. Get to know what your partner needs.

3. Let your partner know how you need to be taken care of when you are upset, sad, or frustrated.

4. Practice not taking anything personally with your partner.

5. Learn how you can best support your partner's purpose.

6. Make time to be alone with each other.

7. Be attentive to your partner's needs. Try to identify where they need your help. If you are unsure, the best thing to do is ask.

8. Be open to hearing criticism from your partner. Learn to ask what you can do better in the relationship.

9. Love yourself.

CHAPTER EIGHT
LETTING GO

POSITIVE AFFIRMATION: *Today I am making the decision to let go of the things that take away my peace. I will let go with love and gentleness.*

The concept of letting go sounds easy but, in practice, can be one of the hardest things to master. How do we let go? What happens after we do? In my deepest struggles, there is always a *Me* hanging on to something. Usually it is a mental position that I need to loosen my grasp on. Whether it is a physical object or a mental position in our minds, the same principles apply to letting something go.

> *In my most peaceful moments, the first and last thing I did was "let go."*

WHAT IS KEEPING US FROM LETTING GO?

There are many reasons why people do not let go, including the fact that they do not realize what they are hanging on to. Is your life being controlled by your mental positions or your possessions? Ask yourself: What has power over me? What can I not live without? By asking these questions, you are stepping back and evaluating your relationship with what has power over you.

This is the first step in letting go of a possession, behaviour, or mental position. Real change happens when you are truly motivated to let go. It confirms that you have the power to make changes in your life. How do you identify what has a grasp on you? You could start by being willing to confront what is controlling you, like habits and addictions.

For example: Do you need three coffees before you can function in the world? It is great to wake up slowly, but when you create a belief that you cannot wake up without carrying out your morning ritual, then you have crossed a healthy boundary. Once you have looked at your bigger habits and addictions, you can move onto the smaller issues that may have a subtle grasp on you. Some of your smaller issues you may not be aware of until you take some time to reflect. These include your smaller quirks and beliefs that run on automatic in your mind. Another way to identify what you may be hanging on to is to look at your comforts. Your supposed requirements to feel comfortable may be the very things, behaviours, or mindsets you most need to let go of.

FEAR

Fear is not an uncontrollable force. When you talk about your fears as if you are powerless over their grasp, you create an unhealthy relationship with them. Besides, you do have the power to overcome your fears. When your fears are out of balance, you feel out of control. The more you are consumed with fear, the less empowered you will be. When your mind is consumed by a fear, that fear feels real. Your mind cannot see the difference between fantasy and reality. If you ruminate on a fear, you can experience it as if it is really happening.

It is much easier to abandon a fear if you catch it early. The longer you ruminate on a fear, the more disempowered you become. Over time, your fears can slowly change your perception and block you from seeing the truth. They can take away your freedom and slowly imprison you in the process. Larger fears have the power to render you completely powerless if you allow them to take over your mind. It is important to work at changing your relationship with your fears. The main thing is that you keep moving forward and away from being disempowered by them. Take small steps to move away from your fears.

For example, if you have a fear of driving, just sit in the car, turn on the ignition, and move the car back and forth in the laneway. With each attempt, do a little more to move beyond your fear. It is also helpful to take some time to look at how you came to have your fear. Once you know how your fear was created, work at letting go of your thoughts around your fear. Break it down for yourself in a logical manner. Ask yourself: Is what I'm afraid of happening now? What are the chances of my fears coming true right now? These are just a few suggestions for you. Come up with your own ideas to help you move away from your fears.

Historically, the people who enjoy success in life are the ones who took risks that others were not willing to take. Being fearless gave them the strength they needed to go where others could not. Observe how fear limits you and keeps you from what you really want in life.

> *Fear and fearless are neighbours. They*
> *live directly beside each other.*

Moving beyond your fears can sometimes be a short trip, because your fears can have a way of looking much bigger than they really are. The key is to take the first step. If someone shared their fears with you, you may think, "Wow, that is such an insignificant thing to be afraid of." The same could be said about your fears, the ones holding you hostage. People have many reasons to support their fears. Letting go of a fear may require you to let go of all the memories associated with it. Be aware of when a fear comes up, and then walk through it. This simple exercise can liberate you from the burden of holding on to your fears.

Freedom lies on the other side of your fear. Once you walk through those fears, you may realize that the fear itself was more torturous than the object of it. Each time you let go of a fear that is holding you down, you will feel lighter and more at peace. Fear robs you of your peace and drives you deep into the shadow of your ego.

Mary Kay, the founder of Mary Kay Cosmetics, the sixth largest marketing company in the world in 2015, was a huge advocate of empowerment in women. She said: "Feel the fear and do it anyways."

Illogical fears are a gross adaptation of your mind. What starts in your mind as a fictional story slowly becomes a matter of fact to you when fear takes hold. Once this happens, you no longer see the truth. You are blinded by your fears.

Fear itself is nothing more than an emotion that is accompanied by a belief. Many fears are not logical and are born out of the fallacies of the mind. Some of my greatest growth opportunities have come from walking through my fears. When you have the courage to overcome your fears, you then have a recipe for overcoming other obstacles in life. Fear can hold you tightly in its grasp. It will take courage and willingness, but you *CAN* overcome even the deepest of your fears.

OVERCOMING FEAR REQUIRES SEVERAL THINGS

1. A willingness to release the voice in your head.

2. The courage to face your fear and walk through it regardless of how you feel.

3. A willingness to let go of your emotions.

4. The willingness to keep moving forward after you have made the decision.

My friend, Kristi Rockley, says: *For your authentic growth and healing, you sometimes need to lean into what is uncomfortable.*

Fear impedes healthy growth; be willing to be fearless and walk through whatever scares you. Staying in your comfort zone encourages repetition of old habits and will not lead to the discovery of your deepest joy. It may actually become your excuse to keep playing small. An empowered person is liberated from illogical fears. Their imagination no longer has control over them.

WORRY

Worry diminishes your power and hijacks your mind. It is also debilitating, for it embeds your fears deep into you. Often people will claim that it is their job to worry and, by doing so, they believe they are helping a situation. In fact, they are not helping whatever situation they are in at all. Worries do nothing to fix a situation. At best, worrying makes you feel heavy and more burdened. Some worries are just the way we project our old wounds onto a situation. For example, if we were mistreated when we were vulnerable, we may project our worries onto any situation in which we see vulnerability.

Worrying about others indicates that you think you know what is best for someone else. You can pray or wish for good things to happen for others, but you need to be aware not to let your good nature disempower you in the process. Worry is an easy trap to fall into, especially when you care about the person in receivership of your prayers. It is helpful to remember that if what you are worrying about is out of your control, then that is an indication that you may need to let go of the thoughts in your mind. Do not allow the worries in your mind to divide you from your true power. Replace your worries with thoughts of love. If you are concerned about a person or situation, send love. This invites the providence of God. The part of you that is made in Gods' image has the power to help and heal the world. Use your power wisely. Love expels your worries and fears.

STRESS

Stress is a huge problem in the world today and begs the question: Are we more stressed than previous generations?

Stress rapidly takes over people's internal experience because it is complex and has many referring factors. One factor is that people today are living through their minds, not taking enough time to rest in the presence of their hearts.

Here is an exercise that can help you rest in your heart:

1. Spend an entire day being heart-centred.

2. When you notice that you are in your head thinking, gently return to resting in your heart.

3. Move your attention to your heart area.

4. Allow the expansiveness of your heart to open while you do this exercise.

Be aware that the mind will keep a steady stream of things to do, to want, and to strive for. This leaves you with little chance to relax and cultivate a relationship with the peacefulness found when resting in your heart.

Often you know why you are stressed, but your fears keep you from making the changes necessary to let go of stress. Make an action plan to remove those stresses from your life. Be willing to make the changes necessary to relieve yourself from your stresses. Remember: You are nobody's saviour

Stress is not created by the events occurring in your life. It occurs as a result of your emotional response to those events. Stress is generated when your emotions flood your body. If you could block yourself from feeling, stress would subside immediately. The good news is that there are several ways for you to manage your emotions. By managing your emotions at the onset, stress does not build up in your body. For when we are full of stress, the smallest incident can suddenly cause anxiety in you.

One of the interesting things about stress is that our minds can create imaginary situations, and then we play them out as if they are real and in the moment.

Of course, you have many valid stresses in your life. But your body is not biased and does not know the difference between valid stress and the stories and stresses you create in your mind. The response is the same whether your stress is real or imaginary. Be open enough to see how your life unfolds in real time versus trying to predict hypothetical outcomes that are mostly created out of fear. When you notice your stress is on the rise, ask yourself whether you are stressing over something that is real. If what you fear is not happening in that moment, try to set down the thoughts and feelings you are having. Just pull your attention away from the feeling and allow it to be there in you. The feeling that is going through your body is not you. It is just a sensation in your body. Let go of any need to defend your feelings.

TIME AND CONTROL

Feeling as if you do not have enough time and feeling a loss of control greatly contribute to stress. These are by no means the only contributors to stress in your life, but they are two big players in the arena of stress.

Slowing down and giving yourself time to breathe can reduce the pressure you place upon yourself. If you feel that you do not have enough time in your days, maybe it is time to take a deeper look at what has your attention.

According to www.hackernoon.com, the average person spends four hours a day looking at the screen of their smart phone. That equates to 1,456 hours per year. If you are awake for sixteen hours a day, that means you have given your phone one quarter of your day. How much time do you spend on your phone? Do you waste vast amounts of time on trivial pursuits?

It is important to give yourself over to fruitful endeavours. What is fruitful for you? It could be something as simple as going for a walk with your partner. Being present with the moment ends the time you spend on meaningless activities that sap you of your time and energy.

Feeling out of control also adds to stress. But look at what you feel you need to control. Are you a micromanager? There is very little that you can control in your life. No amount of needing control can change the wait time in a checkout line or the weather. Life seems to be speeding up for all of us, and the expectation of how fast things should come is at an all-time high. People used to say that patience is a virtue, but today you could say that patience is a rare quality. The sooner you let life be as it is, the sooner you can rest in your peace.

Tolerance can help when you feel that life is out of control or that you need to control what is happening. Your need to control only briefly satiates your ego so, with tolerance, you will find and accept the humanity in others. You open the door for deeper and often unexpected experiences to unfold. These experiences are often positive in nature. Tolerance is just the right button to push when you feel you have had enough.

Intolerance only gives you more to let go of inside your mind and prevents you from moving toward your ultimate peace, whereas learning tolerance lets you and others live amicably while inviting equanimity, especially in the amidst of difficult situations. Intolerance feeds selfishness and leads you to believe that you need more than your share. It also forces you to see through a narrow line of vision.

True tolerance is not just a willingness to tolerate another. It is found in your ability to respect other people's differences—their beliefs, the way they express themselves, and the choices they make. However, that does not mean you should be passive. Taking a stand and finding your voice when you need it is not intolerance. Often the hardest things to say hold the most truth. Tolerance will simply help you get your point across respectfully. This will call others to attention when you speak, but only if you're able to truly embrace tolerance.

How Do We Let Go?

Letting go is like dumping a rock out of your shoe. You stop, let it go, then keep walking without looking back. Your hidden power waits for you under all the things you need to let go of.

Letting go is a decision, but it is a decision that may require work from you. Letting go of one mental construct can upset the balance of other beliefs. It may cause you to look at a series of other mindsets or beliefs you are holding, but it is normal to feel unstable when you are changing beliefs and paradigms in your mind. Being willing to keep moving forward and letting go is key.

Your ability to let go may require acceptance. That does not mean that if someone has harmed you they had the right to do so. Your acceptance only represents that something terrible has happened and you have decided to move forward. You may need to accept events that have happened in your life.

Some events that appear to be traumatic and life changing can turn out to be blessings. Sometimes these events happen *for* you, not *to* you. If you are trying to move on from a trauma inflicted on you, forgiving that person may not be your first step. The first step could be to stop the flow of anger toward the person, place, or situation. It is normal to have negative feelings or ill wishes toward another; however, continuing to project these feelings does not help you to heal or grow beyond the level of suffering.

Acceptance starts your process of healing with the situation. Once you stop the flow of negative energy, a space in you opens for forgiveness to naturally arise. The thing about forgiveness is that you are holding nothing over the other person. If you are holding a grudge or holding anger toward another, it only makes you sick and bitter.

As Malachy McCourt said: "Holding a grudge is like drinking poison and expecting another person to die."

When you do not forgive, you are holding nothing more than a mental position. Acceptance can be a direct path toward your healing. By focusing your anger on another, you are giving your power away, which in turn impedes your ability to help yourself. Never think of acceptance as giving up or letting others win. See it as a powerful position of mind that returns you to your peace. *The road home to peace, is love.* If you are wanting to get over a trauma in your life, acceptance is the first step. Acceptance can be the point from which you move forward.

I held myself back from letting go for many years. I repeatedly tried to forgive a person in my life, but I knew I needed to let go of the hurt and trauma I felt first. But I just could not move forward. I was stuck going through the motions of saying I forgave this person, then befriending them, only to push them back out of my life. Then one day I had a flash of enlightenment. I realized I couldn't accept the things that happened to me. In my lack of acceptance, I justified projecting anger and hatred. I felt that if I forgave that person, I would have to allow them back into my life. This was not the case at all. We can accept, forgive, and move on without inviting anyone into our lives. When I learned to accept all the difficult things around my relationship with this person, I could stop sending anger. In doing so, forgiveness happened on its own. I freed myself of the burden I had been carrying for so long. We give ourselves this freedom the moment we choose to accept and let go.

Letting go takes a hero's heart, for the mind can replay your traumas and dramas your entire life.

Just because you let go once does not mean that it will never resurface in your mind. The landscape of the mind changes slowly. By staying vigilant in your practice of letting go, your mind begins to transform. Be patient in the process and be sure to insert love to self as often as you can. You insert love by being gentle and only speaking kind words to yourself when you have a setback. Again, love is the path home. It leads us with sure-footedness along the way.

Letting Go

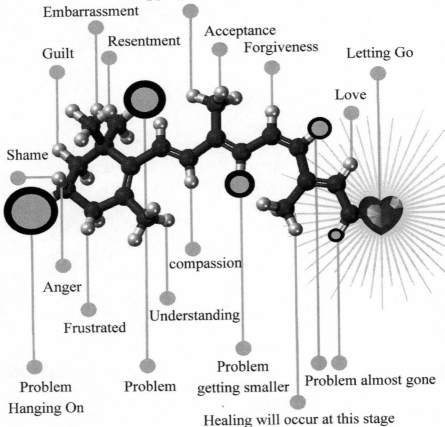

Stopping the flow of anger

Embarrassment

Resentment

Guilt

Acceptance
Forgiveness

Letting Go

Love

Shame

compassion

Anger

Understanding

Frustrated

Problem

Problem

Problem
getting smaller

Problem almost gone

Problem
Hanging On

Healing will occur at this stage

By moving through the stages from left to right, what you
want or need to let go of tends to get smaller and smaller.
Letting go now requires less effort.

DEEPENING YOUR SURRENDER

*In your most surrendered state, the presence of
peace enters your body as a gift to you.*

In the most profound moments in my life, the sense of me completely dissolved. There was no longer any sense of me experiencing the moment at hand; I was just intently present. In this intense moment, I had let go of the burden of my mind and body.

If you look at one of your most profound moments, you might find the same thing. During your most profound moment, you were a witness to what was unfolding in front of you. Even if you were doing something, there was no longer a sense of *you* doing anything.

Being an artist has given me this experience many times in my life. As creation is flowing to and through me, I just become a witness to what is unfolding. While I am tattooing my clients, I surrender and watch the tattoo unfold. This is when the best work happens. For years I had a sense of me doing the work and needing to control everything. I felt that if I let go, even for a second, I would completely botch the tattoo I was working on. What I have come to understand is that quite the opposite is true. The more I allow myself to surrender, the better the outcome. When I watch a new tattooist do their first few hundred tattoos, they usually have a death grip on the machine, as if they are trying to squeeze the tattoo out of it. I would always tell the artists that I trained to just relax, to let themselves go in the process. As they felt more and more confident, I could see them letting go. Once they had mastered this lesson, their work began to take on more life and expression.

Keep letting go until there is nothing left to let go of.

The distractions of your mind's regular activities can steal all your attention in its endless demands. By letting go, you open a space for a deeper interaction with life. As you learn to keep letting go and surrender yourself to your peace within, you begin to stabilize the ability to drop all the things that are driving you away from peace. In your deepest surrender, you discover that peace is ever present in you. All that is required for you to experience it is to let go.

Letting go readies us for the gift of peace to arise in us.
It's not that you obtain peace. It's more like you surrender
to it within and allow it to gift you with a visit.

In this selection of writing by Rev. Safire Rose, she provides great instructions with how to let go.

SHE LET GO

"She let go. Without a thought or a word, she let go. She let go of fear. She let go of the judgements. She let go of the confluence of opinions swarming around her head. She let go of the committee of indecision within her. She let go of all the 'right' reasons.

"Wholly and completely, without hesitation or worry, she just let go. She didn't ask anyone for advice. She didn't read a book on how to let go … She didn't search the scriptures. She just let go. She let go of all of the memories that held her back. She let go of all of the anxiety that kept her from moving forward.

"She let go of the planning and all of the calculations about how to do it just right. She didn't promise to let go. She didn't journal about it. She didn't write the projected date in her Day-Timer. She made no public announcement and put no ad in the paper. She didn't check the weather report or read her daily horoscope. She just let go.

"She didn't analyse whether she should let go. She didn't call her friends to discuss the matter. She didn't do a five-step Spiritual Mind Treatment. She didn't call the prayer line. She didn't utter one word. She just let go. No one was around when it happened. There was no applause or congratulations. No one thanked her or praised her.

"No one noticed a thing. Like a leaf falling from a tree, she just let go. There was no effort. There was no struggle. It wasn't good and it wasn't bad. It was what it was, and it is just that. In the space of letting go, she let it all be. A small smile came over her face. A light breeze blew through her. And the sun and the moon shone forevermore."

— *Rev. Safire Rose*

TOOLS TO DEEPEN YOUR EXPERIENCE OF THIS CHAPTER

1. Make a list of the things that have power over you. In this list, include what you cannot live without.

2. What are your comforts? Do you have rituals you must follow? For

example: Do you need to have three coffees before you think you can function? This is how a comfort controls you.

3. Look at your fears as if they are not yours. Write down how this changes your thoughts about the fear you are viewing.

4. Can you think of any examples where fear has distorted a truth you hold?

5. When you made a list of your stresses, were there any that were not real? Watch for this when you feel stressed. Are you stressing over real things, or future things?

6. What does a typical day entail for you? Do you have things that sap your time and energy? Try to become more conscious of what's draining all your time.

7. Are there things you have a hard time accepting? Make a list of the things you find hard to accept. Once you have your list, you can begin to allow acceptance with the things on your list. Some things may take a great deal of courage and love to bring acceptance into. Just do your best and love yourself during this process.

Seeking the Next Level

The next chapters of this book are dedicated to the serious seeker. I challenge you to let go of the preconceived concepts in your mind if you choose to proceed from here. You will find that I use the word "God" more frequently in these later chapters and, for the sake of extracting the most out of this material, you may be required to let go of what the concept of God has meant to you. To be clear, when I refer to God, I am not talking about religion. I am talking about God in a loving sense. God is not a religious concept. God is the source of all things seen and unseen, known and unknown. God is the totality of all that IS. The entire point of awakening is to know your relationship with God. When you know who and what you are in relation to God, insignificant behaviours, mindsets, and desires fall away as you discover God's presence within you. For convenience, I refer to God as "He." I see the presence of God as fatherly in nature.

Lectio Divina

In the early monastic life, the monks would employ a technique called Lectio Divina, otherwise known as Holy Reading or Divine Reading, as a method of deepening their studies. To get the most out of the following chapters, I suggest that you read them on a deeper level than with your mind. Rest in your heart while you take in what is being presented.

Tools for Deepening Your Study

1. Read the material slowly, savouring the words. Be very present as you

read. If you feel you need to stop and contemplate the writing, don't hesitate to do so.

2. Pause to reflect on how the writing reflects on your life. How can you relate your personal life to the writing you are taking in?

3. The next stage is to open your heart in order to comprehend the reading with your soul and not your mind. Experience the writing and take in the energy behind the message.

4. The last step is to listen to your soul. Does it have any deeper reflection about the material you are taking in?

Note: The above description of Lectio Divina is my own interpretation. If you would like to learn more about this sacred practice of study, feel free to do your own research. Thomas Keating provides some great instruction on the topic.

Chapter Nine
Finding Our Purpose

Positive Affirmation: *My life has great value and purpose, and I am capable of fulfilling both.*

How does one find one's purpose in life? This is a question that had me chasing my tail for many years and almost always caused me pain. I had a feeling that my life was on pause and I could not move forward until I knew, in intricate detail, what my purpose was so I could start my life. I thought finding my purpose was going to be a defining moment in my life, as if God would separate the clouds on a rainy day and speak to me in a grand voice.

I also thought that once I knew my purpose, I would have clear instructions on what I was to do with the rest of my life, and I sought out great teachers and seers to help me. I assumed that everything that had happened before I found my purpose was preparing me for what I needed to know and, once I knew what my purpose was, every moment thereafter would be defined as "After I found my purpose." But the whole concept was just a fantasy that my mind had created, and the teachers and seers could only give me just about as much information as I already had.

As a culture, we start asking children at a very young age the big question: What are you going to do when you grow up? This question was asked of me hundreds of times during my youth but, at age nine, the only thing I wanted to do was build forts in the woods and effectively not get caught peeing outside. This repeated questioning landed a belief in me that I should know what my purpose was right from birth and, because I did not know the answer, that question tore at my self-worth. Within the question is an underlying pressure that we must *do* something.

In the end, nobody had the answers I was looking for. I needed to change my approach and look in a different direction.

THE SEARCH FOR PURPOSE

I count myself privileged that I found my career at an early age and, for years, it seemed that I had found my place in life and that I was well suited to my vocation. By my early twenties, I had acquired all the material things that one would want in a normal middle-class life. I owned my own home, a car, a vacation property, and had filled my life with a great many meaningless objects.

However, under the surface, I still questioned myself. Am I fulfilling my true purpose in life? Even with all these things in place, I still could not help but wonder: Is this all there is? Is this what my life is about? I was haunted by these questions. As comfortable and great as my job of being a tattoo artist was, it did not feel like my ultimate purpose. It felt like I was putting in time until I found what I was really looking for.

In my mid-twenties, though, I had what I would call a spiritual crisis. Nothing and nobody I had met thus far in my life seemed to have the answers I was looking for, so I decided to turn to spirituality. I read tons of self-help books, met some interesting people, and studied all kinds of religions and philosophies from different cultures of the world. After investigating and studying, what seemed to have the greatest allure to me was meditation.

In the end, after all that, I still had not found an answer to my question. The strange thing was, it did not seem to bother me as much. Spirityalty was a great distraction. Eventually, I gave up my pursuit of finding the answer.

Then one day it all became clear to me. Each step of my journey was my purpose. I had finally discovered what I had been looking for most of my life. My life was already full of purposeful moments. There was no great epiphany that was going to tell me what my ultimate purpose is. At every twist and turn of my life, I was automatically fulfilling my purpose when I learned to stay present with the moment and serve what was in front of me. I discovered that our purpose is ever-changing according to the moment we are in.

By placing our attention to the moment at hand and responding to what is in front of us, we automatically fulfil our purpose. There is no longer a question of whether we have a purpose or what that purpose is. We have all kinds of purposes. Life is full of opportunities to fulfil our purpose from one moment to the next.

Instead of our purpose being one giant thing, it is made up of all the endeavours we engage in. The questions we need to address are: What am I drawn to and what excites me? Do my pursuits have purpose to me? We all have a myriad of things that we are naturally good at, and there is a good chance that what we are really good at is all part of our purpose in life.

LIVING ANOTHER'S PURPOSE

Never settle for a life that is less than purposefully yours.

It is not uncommon for us to live another person's life. Our family and friends can have a huge influence on what we do or do not do, and what we are exposed to often has an impact on the choices we make.

We search for our likeness in our circle of friends—that's what usually draws us to befriend another. Once we find a person who shares a common trait, we then align ourselves as friends. But often our friends will expect us to stay the same or, at the very least, to not move beyond them or be different from them. The problem is, we sometimes outgrow our friendships and begin to curb our needs in order to meet the approval of others. This behaviour can cause us to fall into the trap of living another's purpose and can bear even more validity when the person we have outgrown happens to be our partner.

For years I tried to live my parents' life. I started to follow in their footsteps rather than my own. The longer I worked at doing the same type of work they did, the more discontented I became. In my heart I knew what I was doing was never going to get me where I wanted to be in my life. In fact, part of the angst I was feeling about finding my purpose came from not being honest with myself. I was going against what I knew was right for me. I was living another's purpose, and I was going against my own heart's wisdom. It was a recipe for clinical depression.

MOVING TOWARD OUR PURPOSE

Our purpose in life is to live. I mean to *really* live. If someone came up to you and asked: "How do you live a full and purposeful life?" what would you say? Your answer to that question would be the answer to what your purpose is.

I consider my dreams to be like movie trailers. They are previews of what I can live if I choose to live my dreams. Yes, I did say "choose." If you think life is hard for you, you are right. Life is hard. The real question is: When do you plan on changing that?

The answer: When your life hurts enough, you will change it.

This anecdote about a dog lying on the nail by Les Brown illustrates my point.

THE DOG ON THE NAIL

There was a young man walking down the street and happened to see an old man sitting on his porch. Next to the old man was his dog, who was whining and whimpering. The young man asked the old man "What's wrong with your dog?" The old man said "He's lying on a nail." The young man asked "Lying on a nail? Well, why doesn't he get up?" The old man then replied "It's not hurting badly enough."

> *When the voice in your head says, "I can't," replace that with "I will."*

Our life is meant to be lived to the fullest and we must follow our heart's wisdom. It should not be controlled by our deepest fears, nor should we strive for what we think the minimum life has to offer. History has proven time and time again that the human spirit is capable of just about anything. There is no difference between you and your greatest hero. That is the basic premise of the age-old story of heroism. One sets out on an impossible journey and wins.

As we discovered earlier, one of the ways we discover our peace is by learning how to follow and listen to our heart. The more I stripped away the layers of things that I was not, the more my purpose became more apparent. I now think there was a part of me that was hiding from my purpose, because it meant that I would have to step into my greatness. I would have to let go of all the things that I wasn't. I believed for a long time in this sad and twisted story about myself. I believed that I was not good enough, strong enough, or smart enough. But every one of those negative thoughts was just my mind running away on me and driving me further away from living my purpose. It is not that I needed to find my purpose. I just needed to live my purpose. Inside, I already knew what to do from one moment to the next. I just had to be quiet enough to listen to what my heart was trying to tell me.

How to really live your purpose:

1. 1. Learn how to let go of your thoughts.

2. 2. Follow your heart and listen to its wise instructions.

3. 3. Only live the life that is purposefully yours.

4. 4. Live deeply in this moment and watch for how you can serve the world rather than how the world can serve you.

Living these four steps will not only drive you toward your purpose but will create a meaningful and peaceful life for you. With the inclusion of love in these steps, your life will be full of purpose.

Every great adventure begins with the courage to face the unknown.

Be your own support team in life. Why look to others for encouragement? People won't encourage you to do things that they are afraid of. My time working in a factory showed me that very clearly. "I am going to start my own business," I used to say. To which many of my co-workers would respond, "What about the benefits here? What about the guaranteed paycheque?"

I have a thousand more benefits that come with my current job and lifestyle. As for the guaranteed paycheque, the factory I used to work in is now closed. It is not that other people do not want good things for you so much as they cannot see you doing better than themselves. If they could see a way out of their own situation, they would do what you are doing. Go after your dreams. Start moving forward in your life so you are really living. That is living a truly purposeful life.

Our purpose can materialize more swiftly when we maintain our focus on what we want.

MOVING BEYOND OUR PURPOSE

We have come to this earth to live, love, expand our consciousness, and, most importantly, to awaken our soul. We have a great deal of opportunity to explore this great plane of demonstration. This earth is the ultimate playground, and we were never meant to set borders or find ways to divide ourselves from each other. We are here to live as one, love as one, and grow as one. There is so much purpose in life that is hidden from us. Our purpose is not about extracting worth from the things that we do. It is about our authentic engagement with life.

Rather than: What is my purpose? I think the real question is: How can my life serve a purpose? A purposeful engagement with life involves surrendering and serving whatever shows up in front of us. All that we ever need is on its way to us and could be landing at our feet at this moment.

Wake up daily and ask yourself, "How can I make a difference and an impact on the world?" We ask this question not to be known as a hero but to actually become one. True heroes have no agenda for self. They are much too busy serving the world to spend a second of their time looking at how they are being perceived.

Life will hand us all kinds of unique experiences, some pleasurable and others not so much. As I reflect on the passing tides of my life, I am filled with gratitude for all that I have experienced so far. I sit with great anticipation and willingness to fully respond to the moment I am in. We can count the days that have passed in our lives, but we cannot count the ones that lie ahead of us. Place yourself in the moment you are in so you don't miss a single moment of your life. That way you will fulfill your purpose.

TOOLS TO DEEPEN YOUR EXPERIENCE OF THIS CHAPTER

1. Ask yourself: "What is my purpose?" Write down the things that come to mind when you ask yourself this question.

2. Identify where you may be following in your parents' or a friend's footsteps. Keep in mind that this is not necessarily bad if you are consciously choosing this for yourself.

3. Set aside excuses as to why you cannot live your life. Then identify if you are going against what you really want in your life.

4. Become aware of friendships that no longer serve you. It is not a good thing to banish people from your life, but if someone is holding you back, let them go with love.

5. Answer this question: How do you live a full and purposeful life?

6. Remove all the obstacles that are preventing you from following your dreams. Do you believe in your dreams? If not, why not?

7. Become aware of how often you say, "I can't." Are you willing to have enough courage to replace that with "I will"?

8. Become aware of where are you holding yourself back from living your purpose. Do you have old stories about yourself that might no longer be true?

9. Take notice of how and why you hold yourself back from following your heart. Is it because others won't approve or support you?

Chapter Ten

Unity

PART I: FINDING UNITY WITHIN

Positive affirmation: *The spirit in you enlivens the spirit in me.*

In this two-part chapter, we will be exploring the topic of unity. In the first part, we will explore what unity is and how we can foster a relationship with the consciousness of unity in ourselves and with others. In the second part, we will explore how to create unity within our communities. This is important because, by understanding the concepts of this topic, we benefit not only ourselves but as a community. When we are united, there is nothing we cannot accomplish.

We unconsciously seek to find our own likeness in others, but when we see our reflection in them, it can have different effects on us. We can embrace the likeness we see when it reflects what we want to be or what we admire in other people, or reject it when it reflects what we dislike about ourselves. When we see our own wounds or dislikes about ourselves in others, we often have little tolerance for it.

If unity is only explored within the constraints of our minds, it will remain nothing more than a concept, for the importance and value that unity holds needs to be experienced and not described, and we can only experience unity with others when we embrace the world around us and look deeply within it. We are much better together than we are apart, and unity reveals its ultimate power when it is embraced by an entire community. As our communities grow bigger and bigger, we sometimes lose the unity we once embraced. The desire to know each other and give to each other fades if we are too caught up in our own lives. By embracing the concepts shared in this chapter, we enliven the spirit of unity in our communities.

CLEARING AND FERTILIZING OUR SOIL FOR UNITY TO GROW

The very nature of the spark we carry in our souls seeks to be in unity with others. When we experience solidarity with one another, it evokes memories of our origin. It causes us to remember that we all come from the flame of God.

Knowing our true self, the part of us that rests deep in our soul, will help us understand others. In our quiet moments, we come closer to our souls. By placing our attention to the most silent part within our self, we become open to the possibility of experiencing unity.

To grasp the gravity of this, you must have your own experience. My aim is to inspire you to search for unity in you. What is it that ties you to the world and the people you live with?

Unity is a divine truth. There is a rapid discovery of that truth when we love one another, for love itself lives in the heart of unity.

When you look for admirable traits in another, you are more likely to accept, care for, nurture, and build tolerance toward others. This mindset helps you create a deep connection with people, because the possibility of unity is sparked by connecting with another. When you look for differences in others and pull back from people because of what you find, you diminish the chance of finding the unity that co-exists between you and another.

The only distance between you and I is what your mind creates. By meeting the world with kind eyes and an open heart, you decrease the distance between you and others. This in turn summons the spirit of unity to come and join you. This spirit is the premise of how you can create a sacred relationship. A sacred relationship delivers you into the purpose of joining together with another. It will also lead you to a more purposeful life.

WHAT IS UNITY?

The heart of unity houses many guests.
Contentment is one of them.

Unity is a truth, an absolute that lives within our consciousness. The experience of unity decreases the desire for temporary, external experiences. Unity's formless nature begins to fill the void in us that we have been trying to fill all our life and allows us to experience a deep contentment within. The acquisition of material things loses its appeal when the consciousness of unity begins to gift us with its presence and fills us with contentment and awareness of a greater truth.

Contentment is found on the path to peace. With contentment, you are able to deeply surrender. There is nothing grasping at you, nor are you grasping at anything. You may have experienced many enlightened moments in your life when you feel alive and at peace. The experience of unity can visit you in the same way.

The degree and depth to which you will experience the consciousness of unity cannot be wished or willed into your life. It is truly a gift that's given to you by the grace of God. As a spiritual seeker or someone who desires to be at peace, all one needs to do is keep surrendering and letting go. In your most fearless and desire-less state, unity dissolves your soul into the great cosmic ocean of oneness, releasing you of your karmic ties to this life. You are returned to the oneness of God.

THE LAYERS OF UNITY

Unity has many layers. On the surface, unity can be the spirit that joins us when we gather together as one collective unit. Indeed, the spirit that joins us is the power of unity. By coming together, our potential is greatly amplified. If we unite and love is our purpose, there occurs an even greater amplification of power to co-create the most beautiful reality. Love invites God to be present.

When the consciousness of unity permeates you, a deep
sense of completeness washes over you. It leaves you
desire-less for anything other than This Moment.

The depth of unity does not end there. By going deeper, you will discover that the spirit of unity comes from within. Everything we have already spoken about still holds true, but you learn that it is not an external presence, rather an internal one. At this stage, unity is a consciousness that is embraced. By embracing this consciousness, you dissolve the separateness with the external world and all its parts, which brings about great understanding and acceptance of all things. When the consciousness of unity is embraced within you, it eradicates the "how and why" that your mind projects onto most aspects of life. The experience of unity silences the mind, leaving you with a sense of reverence for life. The need for change is not necessary but still most welcome if it comes. In this state of consciousness, the grace and perfection of life is understood in a much deeper context.

There is no guarantee, however, that an experience of a higher state of consciousness will last or return to you again. Its presence is simply a gift to you. There can never be an unknowing of a truth once it reveals itself to you. Being vigilant in your devotion to God allows deeper states of consciousness to unfold, but it is important to remember that the mind can creep back in and take over with its commentary.

But this is not the end to the depth that unity offers. There is still much deeper one can go. The next stage, though, is total surrender into unity, the total union that some of the enlightened masters would have experienced. It is not something you can will into your experience. It comes as a profound gift to those who have deep spiritual merit, and it can only happen if the appropriate conditions are available within a master. It would require total abandonment of one's ego, and a very high level of consciousness.

The Layers Of Unity

Unity is the spirit that joins us when when two or more gather.

This level of unity is available to us all.

If love is the purpose to unite, there is a greater amplification of our power to co-create the most beautiful things.

This level of unity can be experienced by those who are loving and caring individuals.

The spirit of unity comes from within us, it's an internal presence. At this stage, unity becomes a consciousness we embrace.

This level of unity can be experienced by those who are devoted spiritual seekers.

The last step is total surrender into unity. The separation between you and God dissolves.

This level of unity is experienced by the enlightened masters

UNIFYING YOURSELF WITH OTHERS

The following are a few quotes about unity. They speak to the importance and value of coming together with others and the great power that unity holds and promises us. This is the positive side of coming together.

"Alone we can do so little; together we can do so much."

— *Helen Keller*

"It's not in Numbers but in Unity that our greatest strength lies."

— *Thomas Paine*

"For where two or three are gathered together in my name, there am I in the midst of them."

— *Matthew 18:20 KJV*

The power of unity can have a negative effect as well. It is important to know with whom and with what you are unifying. Be aware. There will be people or groups with whom it would be unhealthy for you to align. Alignment expands beyond the people you are spending your time with. For example: Who do you work for? Does your employer have integrity? Where do you shop? Do the businesses you support treat their staff well? Do they acquire their products in a fair and ethical manner? How do the products and causes you support affect the environment or animals?

People often say that they cannot fix the world's problems, but we can start by looking at our practices and associations. By remaining true to our morals, we can make a difference, for we are no longer unifying with the negative forces in the world. Reserve your power to align with what is found in your heart.

THE SOCIAL MEDIA EFFECT

Social media is having a massive effect on how we connect and communicate, but it has its pros and cons. It can draw people closer and remove the distance between them, and this helps create unity. One of the greatest benefits of social media is how it can reconnect you with old friends, help you make new ones, and find local events. All these aspects are helpful in creating more unity between people.

On the other side of the coin, it is important to have real interactions with people rather than virtual ones. Your presence and time spent with your friends and family holds great value.

Nothing ever stays the same and, for the most part, that is a good thing. But how many social media platforms are needed? When did life get so disconnected that we need to spend our time glued to our phones? Balance is the key. Social media can be a powerful tool to spread positive messages and help bring people together. The world is a wonderful place that is full of interesting people. Make time to engage with them, whether it is a stranger at the mall or the person next to you in a coffee shop. You just never know what you might experience.

UNIFYING WITH GOD

"He who experiences the unity of life sees his own Self in all beings, and all beings in his own Self, and looks on everything with an impartial eye; he who sees Me in everything and everything in Me, him shall I never forsake, nor shall he lose Me."

— *The Bhagavad Gita*

Unifying with God calls you to set yourself down. When you do this, you give God the opportunity to arise in you with all Gods glory. Be alone with God, come to God empty of yourself. In your aloneness with God there is great comfort and unity with God. The many guests in your mind can be very distracting. When you give yourself over to God without distraction, God reveals itself in you. The depth to which you discover your aliveness in God is endless. Dissolve any sense of you in the presence of God. You do this with practice. The idea is to keep practicing until there is no longer a you that is trying.

The barrier to unifying with God is your mind. When your attention is placed on thinking/thoughts, or on anything that is outside of you, you give yourself to whatever has your attention. By making God your only focus, you amplify God's presence in you.

PART 2: HOW TO CREATE UNITY IN YOUR COMMUNITY

POSITIVE AFFIRMATION: *The greatness in me is needed by others. When I share myself, the world becomes a better place.*

In the second part of this chapter, I hope to inspire you through some of my personal stories. My experience with unity consciousness has been liberating.

One of the things I feel we are losing today is our sense of community. In all our efforts to claim our separateness and individuality, we might be taking it too far. We need each other and are better together. There are many ways to create and inspire unity in our communities. By bridging the gap between people, we inspire and create connectedness. We build community. It may take time to see a difference, but no act is too small when it comes to loving the world and other people. Our contributions add more than we may realize.

I encourage you to find your own ways to help create a deeper sense of connectedness in your community. By embracing this concept, we can inspire our community to come together and to love and care for one another.

GIVE TO YOUR COMMUNITY

The first act we do to create unity is to give. One of the hardest parts about giving can be knowing what and when to give. Just give whatever you can from the place you're in. You have more to work with than you may realize. All that is required for you to give is to keep your eyes open and be willing to respond to what is right next to you. When you see someone in need, give. Hold the door for a stranger; pay it forward at the coffee shop; pick something up when someone drops it; hold a fundraiser and donate the money to a worthy cause. The list goes on and on.

This very simple concept will add value to your interactions with your community. A quick and effective way to give is by asking how you can help. This simple question removes the mystery. There are a million ways to give from one moment to the next. If you have skills in any area, use your talents to help others.

Some of my greatest experiences have come from volunteering in my community. I have been a Big Brother and volunteered for those with special needs and in palliative care. Each one of these placements helped me grow as a person and helped support and build my community. The rewards you receive from giving to your community far outweigh what is takes from you.

MY TIME AS A BIG BROTHER

In my early thirties, I volunteered as a Big Brother for several years. It was a wonderful experience for me. I tried to use my time to help my little brothers learn how to connect with their community and to communicate better. When I was invited to a pow-wow by a friend on a reserve in Northern Ontario, I decided to ask my little brother if he wanted to join me. He did, and it was an enjoyable day. We met lots of people and learned a few things. We ate some great food and had a small road trip to boot. On our way back to the main highway from the pow-wow, I had a feeling that we should turn right, even though I knew this wouldn't lead us home. I decided I would leave this decision in the hands of my little brother. I pulled the car over and told him we had a dilemma. I explained to him what my intuition had told me and the problem that it would cause. "We have a choice here," I said. "We can go on an adventure or, if you have had enough adventures, then we could continue home."

He promptly said he was up for the adventure. I did not know how far we would have to go or what we would find in the process, but I too was up for the adventure. I told my little brother that we both needed to keep our eyes open for any signs that might lead us in the right direction. We stopped at an antique mall. Neither of us had any hits there. Next, we stopped at a store and, again, nothing special happened. Then we both spotted a sign for an art gallery. "We need to check this place out!" I told him. As we were pulling into the laneway, the owner, an older gentleman whose paintings were on display in the gallery, was just locking the door. As he starting to walk away, we both stepped out of the car and he informed us that he was closed for the day. I told him it was not a problem and we would drop by another time. But just as we were about to get into the car, the man turned around and said, "Why don't you come in … I'm not doing anything right now anyway."

The gallery had a musty smell that hit us soon as we walked in. When I looked at the dates on the paintings, I found out why. He had painted most of them before I was born. He then led us into another room where there were better paintings, and the smell was better as well. Both rooms contained many nature and wildlife paintings. As we made our way to the back of his gallery, the paintings got much better. The last room we entered, which was bright and sunny, contained his most current works. The room smelled great and the paintings caught my attention. The first thing I noticed was that there was an addition here to the nature scenes he was painting. These works were spiritual and included messages from the Bible, like Jacob's ladder, the burning bush, Jesus, and more. I asked him a few questions, since he was such an accomplished artist, and let him know that I too was an artist. I asked if he had any advice for me. An hour and forty-five minutes later, he stopped talking and I picked my jaw off the floor.

Over the course of our lengthy conversation, his advice was simple, humble, and direct. He taught me about my duty as an artist and how I was to serve people with the gifts that come through me. His instructions taught me how to respect others and to build community with my art. Here are his instructions.

1. Give yourself over to your canvas. I was to surrender to the process of allowing my work to use me as a vessel.

2. Always remain humble in your endeavours, even when a crowd assembles around to watch you work. Don't boast or brag. Always remember that we are just artists and not saving the world.

3. Treat your customers well and make them feel as if they are the most important persons in the interaction.

4. Love being an artist.

After what felt like a divinely inspired conversation, my little brother and I got back in the car. We both knew it was time to come home. This meeting with the old man was truly a gift to us. Those are the kinds of gifts I still carry with me today. By taking the time to interact with a stranger, we both learned some valuable lessons. His instructions covered more than how to be an artist—they were instructions for how to build community.

1. Give/surrender

2. Practice humility

3. Be kind and caring

4. Love

SHOW RESPECT TO ELDERS

Respect all those we meet in the community, especially our elders. By being respectful and kind to our elders, we, as individuals, create and enhance unity in the community. My life has been greatly enhanced by the time I have spent with the older generations. I have gained a great deal of wisdom by being quiet and listening to my elders.

Respecting my elders was a gift my parents taught me. As a young boy, I spent a lot of time with my grandmother. She was deaf, so going to her house was different in some ways. It was very quiet in her home. She didn't have a radio, and the sound was always off on the television. I remember playing cards with her on many occasions, and we would pass notes back and forth to each other. My favourite times, though, were when we stopped writing notes and would just sit quietly with each other. It felt like she was teaching me through the silence we shared. This was her wisdom for me. I learned a great deal about my grandma during these times.

Take time to be with the elders in your life. Be patient with them and willing to learn from the lessons they have for you. Our elders have valuable lessons to pass on to the generations that follow. Age does not guarantee wisdom, but by looking for the best in people, we generally find something to admire and a lesson that can be learned.

Showing respect for others requires the personal strength to remain true to your own moral conduct. If someone treats you poorly, remain true to who you are, even in the face of adversity. This always helps defuse the situation much quicker.

Years ago, the operator of the press I was working on kept turning up the speed until I was barely able to keep up. The longer this continued, the madder I became, until I considered punching my co-worker in the face. But I decided the best thing for me to do was to leave the situation before I did something I was going to regret. I stopped the line and said I had to use the washroom.

I was at war in my mind. I really wanted to go back out and start swinging, but I knew that decision would only lead to heartache. In that moment, I asked myself what I was going to do. Then, in a brilliant flash, a diagram came to mind. I had a choice. The seemingly easier choice was to return to the press and come out swinging, but I knew this would result in an uphill battle that would not serve me well. If I made the right choice and just went back out and did my best with a smile, the rest of my day was bound to get better.

I made the hard choice. I went back out and told my operator, who'd been doing my job since I'd left the press, that I was sorry. I was not being a team player. He looked shocked when he heard my words. The rest of that day we worked together and actually had a lot of fun.

Positive Choice

Making a positive choice can be hard to do. It
takes work to climb to the top. But once you reach
the top, all the hard work is done and it is an easy
slide back down to a neutral space.

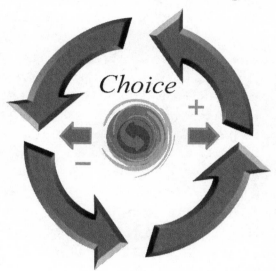

Negative Choice

Making a negative choice can be easy to do. We slide
down with no effort at all. However on the other side of
that choice is a lot of hard work to get you back up hill to
the neutral position.

BUILD TOLERANCE FOR DIFFERENCE

"Beware of the differences that blind us to the unity that binds us."

— *Huston Smith*

In our search for unity, we are drawn to people who share common traits, but it is very important to embrace difference in the community and to search for the goodness in others.

In Jack Kornfield's book, *After the Ecstasy, the Laundry,* he tells a story of his trip to a Buddhist monastery.

Upon arrival, he noticed there were lots of kids and farmers living in the monastery. While being escorted to his room, they informed him that he had to bow to his elders, so he asked for clarity as to who his elders were. He was told they were anyone or anything that had been there longer than he was.

He found it difficult to bow to the kids running around and not respecting the senior monks, or to the farmers who were just sitting out the winter doing nothing at the monastery. However, after a while he learned that bowing was much easier when he found things in others to bow to. When he bowed to the screaming children running in the halls, he was bowing to their youthfulness, and when he had to bow to a farmer, he bowed to the wrinkles around his eyes that were a sign of all the work he had put into mother earth. What he found over time was that there was always something to bow to in everyone he met.

I adopted this mindset years ago, and it has been very helpful for me to learn how to become less judgemental and humbler with my community. I started to look for what I could bow to in people.

I worked for a time as a volunteer with a support service for people with special needs. Ingersoll Support Services wanted to try sound therapy as a relaxation method for the supported, and I was asked if I would come and start a program doing drumming for some people with special needs. I learned more than I ever thought possible from this group of individuals. I committed to one year and, after two and a half years, I could barely peel myself away from the group. Even though this group of people were very different from me, they taught me a lot. They were kind, honest, and real people. They added a great deal of love to my life and taught me how to be more patient, kind, authentic, and how to love unconditionally.

Every week, one of the guys from the group would come to my store. He did this by walking right past his destination (the support services centre where I was doing my volunteer work) so I could give him a ride back, during which we would stop for a coffee and a bagel.

One day I was feeling down in the dumps and had had a very stressful week. I wasn't myself that day and when I looked over at my friend, I could see he was worried about me. Our drive that day was quiet until I asked him, "Can you feel what I'm feeling?"

He said that he could and asked if I was okay. I told him that I was fine and that I was sorry for being so down.

After a few minutes, he turned to me and said, "Ned, how about for today, I will live in your heart and you can live in mine." At which point, I burst into tears.

That young man taught me the true meaning of kindness. He taught me it was okay to not be okay and that just because he and I were very different, we still served a great purpose being in each other's lives. He and I were better together than we were apart. I needed his friendship to inspire me to return to the love in my heart. He needed to give to me and to be my friend that day. I also needed to keep buying this young man coffees and bagels. Clearly, he had gifts to teach me. I have such fond memories of my time with this group. When I reflect on the experiences I had with this group, I now realize that they were a gift from God to me. They came at a time when I needed the most love. I came into their lives trying to make a difference and brighten their days; however, their presence in my life changed me.

SHARE YOURSELF WITH UNCONDITIONAL LOVE

This is a favourite quote from my wife. I love how it reminds me to do my best. *"How you do one thing is how you do everything"* – *Author Unknown*

We all have gifts to offer this world. There is no such thing as a small role here. At times, we play small in the roles we take on, but even in the smallest roles we can play a big part. Make life about sharing yourself, about putting a hundred per cent into whatever you are doing. By sharing our gifts with the world, we actualize our purpose. There are no greater instructions for us in this life than our purpose, for our purpose was given to us by God. It is our special and unique instructions on how to live our life.

Sharing yourself requires that you be present. If you are lost in your mind, you are not giving your full potential to the moment. Have you ever had a friend drop by to visit, but instead of visiting you, they were glued to their phone? Showing up for life means you put down your cell phone and engage in the world around you. Share your thoughts with a stranger, perform an act of kindness. But most importantly, share who you are with others. Show people what is important and special about you.

One of my old friends used to say, "There are hundreds, if not thousands, of people waiting for you to wake up and start living what you came here to do." I believe this to be true. When I have stepped up and really lived my purpose, I have been involved in things that have had a massive impact on my community.

It is everyone's job to help create unity in their community. There is so much to discover in others, more than meets the eye. The greater aspect of what unity holds for us is discovered in the silence we share with one another. It is found in the unseen forces that make up the spark of our soul.

Your life is meant to be a collaborative, co-creating adventure with God and with all of humanity. When you seclude yourself from the world and claim your separateness, you end all possibility of discovering all the benefits of unity. When you turn toward the unity you share with others, greatness follows.

May you embrace the consciousness of unity and be the person who awakens the whole of society. My deepest wish is to inspire you to search for the unity that ties you to the world and all its parts.

TOOLS TO DEEPEN YOUR EXPERIENCE OF THIS CHAPTER

1. For an entire day, try to find something you admire in every person you meet. If you want to take this one step further, after you find something you like about another, let them know.

2. Do you spend enough time talking with people face to face? If you interact more on social media, take some time for real time conversations. A good sign that you are out of balance with your phone is when you are visiting someone and, during your visit, you keep checking your phone or start a conversation on it with someone else. While visiting someone, it is courteous to keep your phone put away.

3. I challenge you to try to start a conversation with a stranger every time you go out.

4. There are many organizations you can join and volunteer with. Be brave and join one in your community.

5. Dedicate yourself to being kind to everyone you meet. Show others respect by engaging with them in a kind and gentle approach.

6. I challenge you to find time to spend with a senior in your community.

7. Next time you find yourself condemning or criticizing another, try to catch yourself and change your thoughts by looking for what you can bow to in them.

CHAPTER ELEVEN

MEDITATION

POSITIVE AFFIRMATION: *I have the power to choose to set my mind down.*

The mind is an elaborate costume we wear. Meditation helps us shed the pieces that are no longer useful to us.

This chapter provides some basic instruction on how to start a meditation practice. Contrary to what you may believe about meditation, there is very little you need to know about it. Meditation is more about the experience and practice of it than it is something we learn and gather knowledge about. There is no need to become an expert on the topic before diving into the practice of doing it. All that is required to enjoy the benefits of meditation is a willingness to set your mind down and focus your attention inward on the quietude of your heart. If you already have a meditation practice, this chapter may help you deepen your current practice by trying different styles of meditation.

WHAT IS MEDITATION?

Meditation has a longstanding history that can be found at the centre of the inner teachings of most religions and many philosophical traditions; however, there are a great many misconceptions around it and how it works.

With meditation, it is easier to describe its many uses and how it affects you than to explain what it is.

Some of the uses and benefits of meditation include relaxation and stress reduction. It is also a tool with which you can change your relationship with your mind. On a deeper level, it can help you discover a vast stillness within you. And deeper yet, meditation can help you create an intimate relationship with God. The depth to which you enter into meditation is different for everyone. It can also be different each time you do it. By the grace of God and your willingness to surrender, you can have many great experiences below the surface of your mind.

The depth of your soul is an endless journey of great wonder.

Of course, this all begins with practice. It is an ongoing experience in your life. Once you start to meditate, you can weave it into every aspect of your daily routine. Meditation can be implemented with eyes open, eyes closed, or even during work and play.

In Chapter One, I discussed how your mind is the greatest obstacle between you and your peace. A daily practice of meditation helps keep the mind in check and minimize its natural tendency to take control and dominate your inner experience. The objective of meditation is not to become a great thinker or to harness the power of your mind. The power of your mind pales in comparison to the power of the stillness found within, for within the stillness of your soul, you find God's image looking back at you.

On the other side of the coin, meditation can stir up old memories, bring about a healing crisis, and land you into dark places. This is not necessarily a bad thing. It is good in the sense to allow yourself an opportunity to heal and move away from the problems of your past. Meditation can provide a safe environment for healing to begin; however, it is a great idea to have supports around you if you find that you are struggling. This is where meditation retreats are a great idea. When you go on a retreat, you make friends with people who are also interested in meditation, and there are usually people around to support you in your experience with meditation.

Through your practice of meditation, you can go as deep or as shallow as you are comfortable with. Superficially, you can enjoy the benefits of relaxation or you can dive deeper into your practice. How far you go in your meditation practice depends on your willingness and devotion, and the grace of God.

PART ONE: MOVING INTO THE PRACTICE OF MEDITATION

*Once you discover who you are, your desire to leave
this moment loses its spark. For only in the presence
of this moment can we know ourselves.*

DROPPING YOUR THOUGHTS

Similar to what we discussed in Chapter One, meditation is not about stopping your mind or its processes. It is about withdrawing your attention from the mind and redirecting it to the quietest place in you. The title of this section is revealing. Dropping a thought can be like dropping a stone out of your shoe. You dump it out and keep walking. The "keep walking" part is the key. Letting a thought go doesn't mean that you drop it for a minute and then go back and pick it up. One of my favourite quotes points to what I am saying here. It is a section from Edward Fitzgerald's translation of the poem, "The Rubáiyát of Omar Khayyam," by Omar Khayyam, 1859.

*"The Moving Finger writes; and, having writ,
Moves on: nor all thy Piety nor Wit
Shall lure it back to cancel half a Line,
Nor all thy Tears wash out a Word of it."*

All that meditation requires from you is to do nothing with the thoughts that arise in your mind. Watch your thoughts like they are a movie, or pretend that they are not real. This may be difficult at times because it is not something we are accustomed to doing. We have been taught that thinking is good and we must keep doing it at all cost.

It's not that thinking is a bad thing, but balance is the key. Being able to use your critical thinking skills is of great benefit; however, when you are finished using your mind, be sure to set it down. People frequently say that they cannot stop thinking. To that I say: "Can't, or won't?"

Our thoughts and what we think about are two different things. Our thoughts come into our mind without any effort from us, while thinking is what we do with the thoughts. We cannot stop thoughts from coming into our mind; however; we can choose what we think about. Thoughts have other associated thoughts attached to them. One thought leads to the next very easily. That is one of the reasons we can find it hard to stop thinking. For example, the colour red leads me to apples, that to apple pie, my grandmother's pie, to eating apple pie, and so on. These loops can be repetitive and get us caught up in our minds.

We cannot stop thoughts from coming into our mind. We can, however, choose what we think about. A good exercise is to be willing to set a thought down mid-stream. When you are caught in a stream of thoughts, try to stop mid-stream. Disengage and let them be.

PART TWO: MOVING YOUR ATTENTION INWARD

Once you loosen the grip you have on your mind, the next step is to learn how and where to direct your attention. There is more to meditation than dropping your thoughts. Once you have learned how to let go of your thoughts, you can direct your attention deeper within yourself.

One technique is to move your attention from your head down to your heart. This may be a different experience for you. Shifting your attention from your thoughts to deeper within can feel very odd, but the more time you spend relaxing, letting go of your thoughts, and surrendering your attention deeper and deeper into yourself, the more comfortable it will become. Why not give this a try right now?

HEART-FOCUSED BREATHING MEDITATION

Bring all your attention to the centre of your heart. Start breathing in and out slowly. As you breathe in, feel your heart expand. As you breathe out, feel it contract.

1. Next, bring up a time in your mind when you felt love. Remember the love you felt and go into the experience and the feeling of that

love. Continue to breath in and out, maintaining your focus on your heart.

2. If during meditation your mind returns to thinking, just pull back from your mind and observe your thoughts as they arise. By not entertaining or grabbing these thoughts, they leave in the same fashion they came to you. The key here is to be gentle and loving toward yourself.

WATCHING YOUR MIND

Another method of meditation is to watch your mind. Watching your mind is like going to the theatre. The screen is your mind, and your thoughts are like the projector shining them on the screen. You don't have to be affected by your thoughts. After a movie, the screen is unchanged. It is not wet from an underwater movie nor is it full of lust from a love scene. When the lights come on, the screen is blank. The same can be true for your mind. When thoughts arise, you can be a silent witness to them. When you learn how to remain unbiased and unaffected by the thoughts you are having, your attention is freed up to be placed inward and rested in the quietest space in your heart.

If you are having a hard time finding a calm and quiet space in which to direct your attention, try starting with a mantra meditation or go back to the focused-heart breathing exercise.

MANTRA MEDITATION

Using mantras can be a very helpful tool to moving into a meditative state. A mantra is a word or sentence that is repeated over and over again. You can say your mantra once and then just rest your attention inward, or you can repeat the mantra for the duration of your meditation. If you only say the manta once and notice you have returned to your thoughts, simply repeat the mantra. Remember, do not beat yourself up for falling back into your thoughts.

You can use all sorts of mantras in your meditations. There are no rules. Make up your own mantra, use positive affirmations, or look up mantras online or on YouTube. As you say the mantra, allow the words to permeate you. The idea is that you are taking your time and bringing your full awareness into what you are doing. It is not a race, nor do you want to be screaming your mantra in your mind. Resist the urge to listen to the voice in your mind. It can run a dialogue during your meditation. For example, as you go a bit deeper, the voice may say, "There you go, you're doing it" or "Is this really working?" Remember, once you start talking in your mind, you are no longer meditating. After you have finished your meditation, take a few minutes to take in the silence. Allow the presence of the silence fill you up.

FIVE STEP MANTRA MEDITATION

1. Make yourself comfortable.

2. Start breathing slowly, in and out, taking in some deep breaths through the nose and out the mouth.

3. Introduce your mantra. Once you feel you are in a rhythm with your breathing, begin to say/repeat your mantra. You can say your mantra aloud or silently.

4. Keep resting your attention on the quietest space you can find in you.

5. When you notice your thinking, very gently introduce your mantra again.

PART THREE: REMOVING THE OBSTACLES

When you sit down to meditate, your mind may throw thoughts at you like, "You don't know what you're doing," "This is a waste of time," "You could be using this free time more wisely," and many others. This is very common, so do not be discouraged by the voices in your head. Just let them go as they arise. Do not to begin to think about them. Just return to your meditation.

When I first started to meditate, I would be meditating and, right in the middle of it, I would start talking to myself. When I caught myself doing this, I would get upset and reprimand myself. Make your mediation practice about loving yourself.

Have no Requirements

Early into meditation practice, I felt that I needed the entire house to be quiet. Next, I needed a special chair, pillow, and music—not too loud but not too soft. Then I needed to sit straight up and burn incense. The conditions went on and on. All of that is a trap. You do not require any special conditions to practice meditation. Just close your eyes wherever you are and begin. If it helps, at first you can go to a quiet room to meditate, but I encourage you not to form a habit of needing special conditions to practice meditation. It is best to practice meditation in all types of conditions and moods. By practicing meditation under all circumstances, it becomes more available to you. Life rarely provides you with perfect conditions to do meditation. Being able to do meditation while your kids are screaming might be the best thing that has ever happened to you.

How to Come to Your Meditation Practice

Sit quietly until the silence becomes a love song in you.

Life reveals its own kind of perfection when we step out of our minds and into the moment. The need to change things gives way to simply allowing what is to be.

Meet your meditation practice with innocence and allow each one to be as it is. Meditations are like snowflakes; every experience is different. Do not allow yourself to place judgements on your meditation. It does not need a critique—good, bad, or middling. Labelling your meditations can only lead to trying to repeat an experience. I have never had the same experience twice during a meditation. The stillness in me has qualities that I am familiar with, but the experience is ever – changing. By removing the labels and the need to recreate an experience, you will keep your mind out of your meditation practice.

Meditation can be done with eyes open or closed, but I would encourage you to do as much meditation with your eyes open as you can. You can apply the same information with your eyes open. Practice this during your day when you are not able to sit and close your eyes. This makes your practice of meditation more of a lifestyle, and it becomes a valuable tool to change your internal experience with your mind. Given the fact that 80 per cent of your thoughts are negative and repeating from those you had yesterday, it might be a good idea to change how you respond to them.

I spent years getting upset over the same topics. I could not imagine having to repeat that experience for the rest of my life. Why be stuck in a terrible mind space? You can choose what you do and what you think.

My heart speaks the loudest when my mind is the quietest.

May your meditation experience be one that delivers you to your deepest peace. Your meditation practice can not only deliver you inner peace, it can also lead you to a space that is full of timeless wisdom.

In one breath, I let go of my mind. I instantly disappeared. In my next breath, I turned toward the silence inside; I suddenly came back to life, full of peace and love.

Chapter Twelve
The Creative Side of God

Positive affirmation: *I invite the power of creation to come and use me as a vehicle to move through. There is no limit to the creative genius that can flow to and through me.*

The Discovery and Awareness of God through Creation

This chapter is about the discovery and awareness of God through creation. You can actually interchange the word "God" with the word "Creator," because God is the ultimate creator. The absolute wonder of creation awaits your invitation. It waits in perfection for you to call upon it to move through you. It is my sheer delight to steep in the trail of dust it leaves behind in me.

As an artist, I have developed an intimate relationship with creation. Creating is not just what I do to make a living … it has helped me learn how to live. Working with my creative side has taught me a great deal about letting go and trusting. The nature of creativity is such that it draws from the unknown and manifests itself into the known. It is a gift given to us. A creative life is an adventure, because you find your answers and directions directly from the source of creativity rather than just recreating the same life day after day. By understanding the nature of creation, you can draw from your creative side. This doesn't mean that you need to be an artist. You need not even be creative to enjoy the benefits of creativity. You only need to be willing to allow creativity to flow through you.

Your ability to channel creativity will help in many areas of your life. It can help with problem solving and decision making. Every aspect of your life, from work to play and rest, can be enhanced by allowing creativity to use you. Working with creativity can become a way to live.

You will notice that I use the word "movement" in this chapter. When I do, I am talking about the creative aspect of God, which moves to and through us. The movement of God is the life force and innate intelligence within all our creations. Creative ideas that come to us are the breath that God breathes into our bodies, minds, and soul. There is equal opportunity in us all to tap into this endless well of creative energy. Creativity lives in everyone; therefore, all we ever need to do is call forth this energy from within.

Calling forth our creative side is about listening and watching. As we learn to get ourselves out of the way, creativity will flow with ease and clarity. In the process of setting ourselves down, we prevent our minds from tainting what is coming to us. In comparison to your mind, which is an overgrown foot path, creativity is a fourteen-lane highway.

Your creations are the completion of God's gifts. That is the very purpose of form. It is the completion of God's expression.

Most creative endeavours begin with an enlightenment—that "Ah! I am going to do this or that" moment. That is the nudge you are given to start moving toward creating. As you begin and sit in front of the great abyss in wonder, you might ask yourself: "How am I going to do this thing that has come to my mind?" The key is your willingness to start. Once you begin to create, the how and why slip away, and you might just get lost in the act of creation.

What is really happening is that you are getting lost in the presence of God. For me, when I am finished a creation, I often step back and marvel at what is in front of me. This is the pure joy of creating. At the end of a creation, you are blessed with the residual effects of the energy of creation that flows through you, the trail of dust I referred to at the beginning of this chapter. It is a wonderful gift you are given.

THE MIRACLE IN MEXICO

During a two-month meditation retreat in Taxco, Mexico, I had an opportunity to take a trip to see the pyramids. I was halfway into my retreat, so a break from the monotony of doing meditation non-stop was inviting to me, and I was elated.

One of the pyramids we were going to see was called The Pyramid of the Sun, and it was located in the archaeological complex Teotihuacan, northeast of Mexico City. It was huge, and the wonderful thing about it was that you could climb up and sit on top of it. I did just that and spent most of my day doing a solar meditation, a mantra that is based on the sun. Fitting, given my location.

We returned to Mexico City around ten o'clock that night and, though my tour guides quickly turned in, I sat there in a bedroom by myself and knew there wasn't a remote chance I was going to fall asleep anytime soon. I was energized from the day and from spending several hours sitting on top of a pyramid. I decided to just spend the night doing meditation. At about 3:00 a.m., the most bizarre thing happened. Like a brilliant flash, I spontaneously became aware of all sorts of information about creation and the Beloved within me—information that was new to me, but it felt like deep and ancient wisdom that has been long forgotten. I then spent the next four hours in awe of what had just happened as my mind raced with my thoughts. I could not wait to get back to the Hacienda in Taxco.

The two-hour return bus ride felt like an eternity, and when I arrived back to the retreat, I went straight to my teacher's house. Before I could say a word, he looked at me and said, "You were downloaded." I started to say that I needed to write what was in mind, but he cut me off and replied, "Not now."

Confused and overflowing with information, I again questioned my teacher. "When?" His response was that I would know when the time was right.

This book contains some of the knowledge that was given to me during that transmission, and my next book will hold even more. I have been writing for the last nine years and, bit by bit, the wisdom I received that night is coming back to me. Some deep truths about creation were revealed to me and, for years, I have remained quiet about what I had in my head—until now. This chapter contains some of what I learned that night.

BREAKING DOWN HOW CREATION COMES

On the path of creation there are no bumps on the road. When you enter God's grace, God paves the way for a smooth ride. It is you that gets in the way and creates all the bumps.

One of the things I have come to understand is that you are not solely responsible for creation. Creation is God's domain. You are the completion of Creation. When an idea comes into your mind, you may think you are seeing the beginning of Creation but, in truth, you are seeing the end of Creation. Ninety-nine per cent of Creation happens in its formless state. The last one per cent is when you complete it here in the physical. Everything has been worked out to complete your creations before you are ever given the idea to create something.

The Sanskrit word *Hiranyagarbha* (pronounced Har-on-ya-garba) means the primal cosmic force of all Creation. It describes what I have just outlined above.

You are the vehicle through which Creation works and, because all the work has been done before you receive the idea to create something, all you ever need to do is surrender and allow it. Like driving, there is very little effort required by you. You start the car, push the gas, and steer. Essentially, the car does all the work. God offers its gift of creation the same way. God pours itself through you. All you need to do is rest and God will do all the work. Allow God to be the Creator as you surrender deeper into creation.

This doesn't mean that you won't have to work hard in your creations. You may have to apply a great amount of effort for your creations to come to fruition. When you devote and surrender one hundred per cent of yourself to the act of creation, you fall into the silent nature of God. In this silent nature, you harness the power of God to create. The realm of impossibility completely vanishes from your mind, and you are given the ability to see a way to complete the most seemingly impossible tasks. By deeply surrendering, you don't take away from the creations that are coming through you. You become a pure and clean vessel through which things are manifested. Creation is like a beautiful dance, and you just follow its lead. It knows where it wants to go. It knows every move and step that is needed for you to create what is being expressed through you.

CREATING WITH LOVE

Love is an intricate part of creation. When you love what you are doing, your connection to God's grace is amplified. It profoundly alters your ability to make a deep connection with God and to channel God's creative power through you.

When you deeply surrender to the process, you then become unlimited in your ability to create. You are no longer creating from the finite nature of your mind; you are creating from the Infinite Space that lies within you. Over the years, I have spent thousands of hours allowing the grace of creation to flow through me. Her silent gifts were waking me up bit by bit. That is one of the extraordinary gifts that creating offers you. It is the gift of awakening. The presence of creation has a way of guiding you into the depths of your soul. When you are witnessing creation flow through you, what you are seeing is the movable aspect of God.

When you embrace your creations with love, you send a special invitation asking God to join you in your creations. Much as love is the currency in relationships, it is the same in Creation. Love adds value and depth to what you create. The more love you channel into your creations, the more value they contain. It is not monetary value that your creations contain as much as a window into God's domain. When your creations are co-created with God, the viewer can see, or, for some, feel, God's reflection in them. This reflection they see or feel has the power to spark an awakening in them, for it can cause the viewer to become aware of their own divinity.

A creation in which God has moved through you can move another. Use your creations to enliven your love and to awaken the spark of divinity sitting deep in your soul. This is how channeling creation can wake you up.

The unique quality of love's expansive nature in our creations is that Love/God touches people wherever they are. Then it opens them a bit further.

Love and devotion create a forward motion in you and can speed up your evolution of your creative abilities. They can also push you over plateaus you find yourself entrapped in. If you find tapping into your creativity a struggle, you may have become too involved in the process. You have separated yourself from God's ability to create through you.

This is an example of how you place bumps in the road that hinder the process. Creation and love have their own well-defined attributes. Alone, each one is full of depth and beauty, but when you merge them together, your co-creative abilities are exponentially increased. Without God, our creativity is limited to the finite nature of our minds and our limited experiences. With the insertion of love into your creations, you tap into the limitless nature of creation rather than trying to force creativity when you execute your creations on your own.

It is natural when you first begin to create that doubt, worry, and fear arise in you. Your mind might want to track, review, judge, and criticize the things you are doing. Do not succumb to this. Abandon these ideas, for they diminish your connection with God and your ability to co-create.

With the presence of God in your heart and mind, your life can be a collaborative, co-creating endeavour. Ponder that for a moment. In your collaboration with God, you can create a life of endless joy and possibility. A creative life is one that never becomes redundant; the nature of creativity is about exploring and expressing. Allow Creation and love to play a part in your life. By allowing this, you will discover God moving through you. The truth is, God is always moving through you. The creative aspect of God is unrolling your life right in front of you, creating the ground you walk on. The direction and speed in which things are coming and changing add great entertainment along the way. You just never know what is around the corner. How and what shows up in your life is determined by you.

MAKING YOUR LIFE A CREATION

Life itself is a creation that gives you many opportunities to do and become whatever you choose. Your life is made up of hundreds of thousands of choices that you make over the duration of your life. In any given moment, the choices you make will set a series of events into motion. Remember, this moment is all of eternity. Everything that is backwards and forwards is included in this moment. As you deepen your consciousness, more discernment is required, for your choices will begin to impact larger and larger circles radiating out from you. By becoming aware that you are creating your life, you will be called to sharpen your focus. This will keep you pointing in the right direction.

You are creating your life. It is not just landing at your feet for no reason. There are many unseen forces that come into play as the result of the choices you make. Who you are creates a field that surrounds you. It reaches out into the world and finds what you are and draws it to you. Once you have this knowledge, it keeps you aware of your trajectory. Wherever your consciousness lies, there are a range of different potentials that can be actualized from that space.

The Choices That
Create Your Life

Unseen results of our

Thoughts
Intentions
Actions
Words

All of your future helps create what is unfolding now

All of your past helps create how your life is unfolding now

Unseen results of our choices

Unseen results of our choices

All the choices we don't make create this moment

Your present choices create your life

Unseen results of our choices

There are a great many unseen forces at
work as a result of our choices.

A VISIT FROM A VERY INTERESTING MAN

I once owned a gift store as a side business. It was an ordinary day when
Tisha, my receptionist, came into my office to let me know there was a
gentleman out front who had some giftware to sell me. His offer piqued my
interest, so I asked her to send him back. When he entered my office, his

warm presence washed over me. He explained that he had owned a section of the Hudson's Bay store in London, and even though he had been out of that business for a few years, he still had some inventory to get rid of. Right away I agreed to meet with him and asked Tisha to set up a meeting with him for the next morning at a location of his choosing.

As soon as he left my office, I had a feeling that he was a teacher or, at the very least, a conscious person from whom I could learn. I couldn't wait until the next day to find out if my intuition was correct, so I excused myself from my client to catch him before he left. I wasn't sure how to phrase my question, so I just blurted out, "Are you a teacher?"

I didn't know if he was going to think I was crazy or if my intuition was accurate. Thankfully, my intuition proved to be right. "Yes, I am," he responded.

"That's what I want to talk with you about tomorrow, and, of course, I will look at your giftware." The man just smiled. The depth of peace coming from him sent me into an altered state, and the look in his eyes gave me a preview of what was to come the next day.

When I arrived to work the next day, Tisha informed me that my first appointment had cancelled. I now had two hours to meet with my guest from the day before. When I arrived at our agreed location, The Olde Bakery Café, he was waiting for me. I had shared the story of our first encounter with a friend who then asked if he could join us. The three of us sat down and I started the conversation with a question. "Could tell me about the Beloved within?"

My friend and I didn't say a single word for the next two hours. During that time, the man talked about many things. He told us that, in this moment, we are living out thousands of potentials simultaneously. Where we show up is where we place ourselves consciously. The specific potential we choose is just one of many potential outcomes for our life. Our path is determined by where our consciousness lies. No matter what we choose, all potentials are happening simultaneously. But this information was a little much for my consciousness to grasp during our conversation that day.

This concept is more scientifically explained in the double slit experiment by Dr. Fred Alan Wolf. You can find Dr. Wolf online at www.fredalanwolf.com, or you can YouTube search "Dr. Quantum Double Slit Experiment."

When he reached the end of his talk with us, I asked him if I could meet with him again. His response was as bizarre and mysterious as his appearance in my life. "If you need me, you will know where to find me. If you don't, it will be like we never met and I never even existed, and you will never see me again."

After he left the café, my friend and I sat there looking at each other in disbelief about the conversation that had just taken place. I asked my friend "What did you think of that conversation?"

He replied, "Which part?"

I named a few key topics from his talk. Strangely, my friend, who had been sitting right beside me hearing everything I was hearing, had missed the entire conversation. It went completely over his head and he couldn't recall a single thing from the conversation. It was a clear message: this man was here to see me, not my friend.

It is only now that I am beginning to understand the things that the man shared with me that day. It never made sense to me why he was talking about our lives as playing out thousands of potentials simultaneously. It does now

Our life is a gift of Creation that happens by the grace and movement of the Beloved in us. The Beloved is the movable, feminine aspect of God. As we create our lives, we choose which potential outcome we would like to experience.

It is the Beloved in you that creates all and the many potentials available that are happening right now. The Beloved is not an outside spirit that comes to you. It is an eternal presence of God living in you. The made-up reality of your ego is not godly, but your soul is made with the eternal fabric of God.

TRAJECTORY

The ultimate meaning of free will is to choose your highest potential that lands you in a conscious life. A conscious life is one that is lived with the grace of God leading the way.

Trajectory is the range of possibilities in front of you. You have many roads that you can choose to travel, ranging from difficult to joyful. The road you are on within your trajectory is based on the choices you make. As you expand your consciousness, the field of trajectory changes with that growth. The more conscious you become, the farther and wider your trajectory expands, allowing your reach to encompass greater goals and affect more people.

You are never stuck in your trajectory. You have the power to change it. Your trajectory changes by becoming more conscious. The more conscious you become in your range of trajectory, the more likely you will be to make a leap in consciousness. One of the fastest ways to expand your consciousness is to make choices that embrace love and service to your fellow humans. Remember, expanding your consciousness is not a linear process. It is actually not a process at all. Your state of consciousness can go up or down anytime.

When you move into a path that embraces truth, you step off the arduous road and place yourself on a more joyful one. This transition happens when your words and actions are in a place of truth and integrity. It is important to know what you are pointed at in your trajectory, for it is a preview of what's to come for you.

Waking Up to Your Potential

With consciousness, one awakened person can move mountains. This means *you* can move mountains. Yes, you! Your path in no less important nor less purposeful than any others. When I was still asleep in my life, it felt hard to make the necessary changes I needed. My definition of being asleep in your life is being a prisoner to your mind and not living your destiny.

It took a great deal of willingness to heal and grow from my dramas and traumas. In my experience, there are great rewards for doing your inner work. The life I was living was much harder than the effort it took to change. I didn't know that I could create my life with God. Now I have no desire for my drama or anyone else's dramas and traumas. By healing my past and retracting my desire for drama, I have learned how to flow with all the things that cross my path. After acceptance and forgiveness comes love. When I let go of my struggles, a new place within me opened. By embracing a loving consciousness, all the difficult things just don't matter.

My only aim now is to be the love that I am, for any other life would be mundane and pointless.

The creative life doesn't mean that we are required to create big things to be happy. It is actually the other way around. Because you are truly content, big things just seem to happen all around you.

The greatest creation you will make is your life. Use your life to awaken yourself and anyone who crosses your path. Leave nothing untouched by your love. I know now that nothing is missing or misplaced in my days. I have always had all the things I have ever needed. If things are missing in your life, it is because you intended for it to be that way.

OPENING MY SHOP

I had been tattooing for about ten years privately in my home when, around the year 2000, I decided to move my business to the business section of my hometown. My next step was to find a store front. At the time, I had met an interesting doctor who was helping me. One of the things he did was teach me a course based on a book called *The Science of Getting Rich*, by Wallace D. Wattles. The doctor had taken the course from Bob Proctor, a teacher in the United States who teaches the law of attraction. The base that he draws from is the "New Thought Movement" formed by a group of really great authors around the late 1800s to early 1900s. The doctor was teaching the course in his office, and it referred to the real richness you get when you can co-create your life with God.

I found the information interesting, so I began to use the principals he taught me. I really wanted to take my business to the next level and do something that was unheard of at the time. I opened a tattoo shop/ metaphysical healing centre/gift shop. I believed so deeply in the idea that I could not see how funny that must have seemed to the public, since some of the healing modalities that I had in my shop were still under the radar back then.

I wanted to buy a house in town that was already zoned for business, but I just could not seem to get a bank to give me the mortgage I needed to open a business like the one I was planning. So I decided I would rent a store. This meant that I would have two of every bill and, since I was living paycheque to paycheque at the time, my partner thought I had lost my mind. Her opinion was valid because, to open my store, I needed ten thousand dollars. I decided that I was going to take a leap of faith and go for it anyway. I just knew what I was doing was right for me, so I went ahead and signed a lease, not knowing how or where I was going to get my start-up funds.

Three days after I signed the lease, I was in the bank renewing the mortgage on my house and, during the process, the banker looked up at me and said, "Do you need any money?"

"Yes, I do," I said. "I could use ten thousand dollars."

"I think we can do that," she replied.

I looked at my partner and just smiled.

What I learned from the course the doctor taught me was that there is a creative force in the universe that you can draw from and co-create your life. It creates what you image in your thoughts, but you must expel any disbelief from your mind. Your belief needs to be so strong that you begin to practice gratitude before you even receive the thing that you want to create. I claimed my power to draw to me all the things I needed to create the new life I was going to live. When I did, the universe couldn't help but respond.

The other component to this story was that when the first option did not work out, I did not tuck my tail between my legs and run away. I looked for how I could make my dream work. I followed my heart, even when the information it was giving me didn't seem logical. I trusted and it did not let me down. The creative intelligence was wiser than I was. All I had to do was listen and trust.

"*The mind of the experiencer creates all the objects which he/she experiences while in the waking or the dreaming state.*"

— *Shankara, Crest-jewel of Discrimination*

You are a divine being here on earth. Know that it is your birthright to create while you are here. When you can let go of who you think you are, a glimpse of your true potential is revealed. You are powerful beyond belief. Use this knowledge to create the most beautiful life for yourself. Know that the most beautiful creation you will ever create is the destiny of your soul, for it is the most perfect creation that is available to you. It is already here and it is fully formed for you. Completing your destiny only needs your consent.

TOOLS TO DEEPEN YOUR EXPERIENCE OF THIS CHAPTER

1. Do you have any blocks with your creativity? You may be more creative than you think. Make a list of all the things in your life that require you to be creative. Try to see how creativity is already in your life.

2. Practice letting go of your mind while creating. This will help creativity flow better.

3. Think of every thought, feeling, or action you make as a creation that is making your reality. Keep this in mind as you go about your day. Watch how the things you have your attention on move into your life.

4. Take some time to look at what is in your range of trajectory. Where are you pointing? What have you put yourself in alignment with? The answer is your trajectory.

Chapter Thirteen
Free Will Versus Willingness

POSITIVE AFFIRMATION: *With a clear and earnest heart and mind, I direct my will to create harmony in my life.*

Free will is the choice we make to choose whatever path we want to pursue. But with choice comes responsibility. Before you make impactful decisions for your life, ask yourself: "Does this serve my soul, or am I fulfilling a desire?"

Free will can be tricky to manage, fun to play with, and potentially dangerous if it is mishandled. In an effort to escape life unscathed, my greatest struggles have come from exercising my free will; however, there can be order to our struggles as well as our joys. The mind projects its opinion onto life's experiences with sheer ruthlessness. It does not understand the larger context of life.

Conversely, I don't believe free will gives us permission to wildly chase our desires, nor is it right for us to force the world around us to comply with our minds' opinions in an effort to satisfy our egos. Our soul is an unbiased witness to life. Its nature is free and unattached to all of our endeavours. Chasing desire is a fruitless pursuit that bastardizes the purpose of having free will. The will of my soul is very different from the will of my mind. My soul understands the duties I have agreed to and is impartial to them. In my position of being impartial, I am able to commit to my duties with fewer interruptions from the demands of my ego.

SURRENDERING THE WILL OF YOUR MIND

By surrendering your will, you may set forth a flurry of action in your mind. The very idea of surrendering your will is counter intuitive to the infrastructure of the mind/ego. The mind has a built-in contingency plan for survival, and any sign of abandoning it sounds an alarm to your ego. The ego has no tolerance for surrender, because surrender is the beginning of the end to its existence.

Surrender may seem like you are giving up, but it is actually turning your attention to your source of true power. It opens the possibility to hear your soul's guidance. This guidance may be simple and direct—so simple that, at times, you may invalidate the wisdom in it. It is your mind that wants things to be more complicated than necessary.

Some of the greatest truths are very simple. One of the greatest being love. Love is a simple truth that everyone understands. It is your mind that makes it complicated. Following love offers simple and effective guidance that is divine in nature.

DOES GOD HAVE WILL?

Where does God fit into all this, and does God actually have a will? During one stage of our consciousness, we appear to be a separate fragment from the Divine as we experience being human. But as we transcend into deeper states of consciousness, the dichotomy between us and God disappears. God and the "I" are no longer two things. There is only one thing, and that is God.

God does not require or want petty things from us. Nor is there a God sitting out there wanting to control our life. By giving our Creator humanistic traits, we reduce God to fit into our mind and reduce the Omniscient to the finite nature of being human. This is nothing more than a fantasy of the ego as it tries to weigh and measure what is beyond measure. Understand that when it comes to the will of the Divine, it is something that is carried out over the duration of our life. God's will plays out through those little nudges we get to turn left or turn right, take a job or leave a job. Not every decision is from the will of God, but the ones that we make from our heart and soul are Divine in nature. Learning how to discern where our will is coming from is a matter of learning how to be in touch with our soul versus our mind.

Our destiny is actualized by allowing God's will to manifest through us. For God's will is the destiny of our soul. Once we realize that God's will, and the soul's purpose/destiny, are one and the same, we then surrender to God without the opposition of our mind. As we unite into God's will, God's grace enters our lives, gifting us with divine favour. Creating God's will is the work of the soul. It is also what brings us into union with the true self.

The will of the Divine moves through us always. Nothing is outside of God. Our life in not a singular linear event played out over the duration of time. It is a multi-dimensional occurrence playing out in all of time. Our soul continues until it has communion with the Divine, at which point it dissolves into the oneness of all.

No matter how chaotic you think life is, there is order to the world. As you expand your consciousness, the order of life is more evident. Within this understanding there is peace, not turmoil, in contemplating the not knowing how or what is to come next. Next is not important. What is important is to surrender your will and allow a deeper awakening to unfold in you, now. In that awakening, there are many beautiful, partial truths to abandon. The will of your mind may be one of them.

THE GRACE OF GOD

We do not walk this path alone; the grace of God plays a significant factor. God's grace is a gift we are given. With devotion and intention, we call upon God to weave Itself into our lives. The grace of God is always at work; however, we may not be aware of all the miracles taking place. As we grow in consciousness, so does our awareness of God's grace unfolding within and around us. Our job is to look toward our soul or toward love. God moves the rest of the way to us. As our devotion and willingness to surrender to our soul increases, grace becomes like a tidal wave, moving all that is required of us to effectively fulfil our soul's purpose.

THE WILLINGNESS TO SERVE THE WILL OF MY SOUL

In an effort to serve the will of my soul, I have surrendered the will of my mind. I have turned my life over to God. Although this may sound like I'm giving up my life, it couldn't be further from the truth. I am claiming the life that was destined to be mine. This is the best life available for me. In you lies all the prophecies of your life. It is all written for you. It is found in the will of your soul, and your heart is the doorway. By following your heart, you know what to do. Following the heart isn't a difficult or a hidden road. You will be guided every step you take. There is a knowing in you as to what you are here to do. By making the choice to enter the path laid out for you, you become the right hand of the Divine. Free will is no longer the object of your affection. Free will is now surrendered and replaced with a willingness to surrender, to "being willing." Living your destiny only requires your willingness to surrender and keep surrendering yourself to your soul.

True surrender is more than just letting go. To deepen your surrender, you make a covenant with yourself to surrender your body, mind, spirit, and soul. In that surrender you become willing to do whatever it takes to follow through with soul's guidance. Anything less than one hundred per cent commitment signals lack of trust, thereby giving fear the power to reside within you. This new position creates a deeper commitment to your soul's purpose and delivers you into a living relationship with your soul.

One of the mind's commentaries that disables your ability to surrender is, "I know, I know, I know." It runs like a tape loop because your mind thinks and believes that it knows everything. This renders you less capable of surrender. The constant bombardment of "I knows" in your mind interrupts the moment you are in and keeps you stuck in your head. In surrender, you admit that you don't know and that you are open to be guided by your soul. There is nothing left on the level of the mind to explore. We receive guidance from our soul by moving outside the context of our mind. By doing so, the guidance deep within us gets louder and clearer. This positions you to dance with the unknown and live life as an adventure with God, returning you to your natural state of innocence. You may know about a lot of things, but just because you know about something doesn't mean you have exhausted your learning on the topic.

From the perspective of "being willing" (surrendering to the will of your soul/God), you allow and accept what is present in your path without the need to reject what is meant for you. This allows you to see a much deeper reality playing out all around you. The order and perfection become more obvious as your relationship with your soul grows. It does not make the evils of the world less tragic or right—it just positions you to move beyond your problems more swiftly.

ADDING DEVOTION TO SURRENDER

*Ceaseless staying with God is the deepest
devotion you can offer God.*

If everyone started to follow their destiny, this world would be a much different place. You would be experiencing the Kingdom of Heaven here on earth. Surrender removes the struggle with life. With true surrender, you find yourself in a much deeper place of devotion—a devotion to the Divine in you that is solid and stable. By giving your devotion to your soul, you have a place to direct your attention. You no longer need to look outside of yourself for the guidance you need in your life. You move into what I refer to as "ceaseless staying with God."

This is the gateway to entering heaven on earth. Passing through this gate places you into an entire new dimension of your soul. Heaven on earth is more than a possibility; it is a solid and stable reality that is here now and meant for you and me to discover. It is a dimension in yourself that can be discovered by anyone who comes to it with an earnest heart and a persistent will. It is not a faraway place that is inaccessible or revealed to a chosen few. It is for everyone to enter and explore. The concept that heaven and hell are what come after your life here on earth is not the whole truth. Heaven and hell are here now. We will continue to experience both until we wake up to our soul. Once we know the depth of the soul within us, heaven and hell disappear, and we move on to eternal life. Heaven and hell are temporary results of the karmic path we walk upon this earth, whereas the soul is the eternal life of God. (I'm getting ahead of my self here. I have borrowed some of this from my next book.)

When you surrender to your soul, a fire within you ignites. When you add devotion to your surrender, it is like adding gas to that fire. Your devotion to surrender means that you are surrendered with love. Your surrender is not a onetime event either. It is ongoing and applied many times a day. At times you may not even know if what you are doing is working or making a difference, but stay true to your practice. The part of you that is in question is your mind—not the true you.

THE WILL OF GOD'S LOVE

The will of God's love is forever accessible. There is never a time when you are beyond its reach. Consciously surrendering your life to your soul's will makes your life an instrument of God, causing you to be the right hand of God. Becoming an instrument of God positions you as close as you can humanly get to the brilliance of God's love. It illuminates the path you are on and removes many of your struggles. With great persistence to execute your soul's will, you place yourself on the path to experience a depth of love that you have only dreamed about. It is a love that is so pure that being in its presence nourishes your soul for eternity. Let the grace of God's love remove all doubt in you. By doing so, it makes anything possible.

The fastest way to experience love from the Divine is to give your consent. By inviting God to be with you in your life, God's love can work more freely through you. This is your choice. It is not one that you should be bribed into. God has no desires for you. Your consent must come freely, not through fear of consequence that you will be punished if you do not consent to God. Fear has no place in your relationship with the Divine. According to Thomas Keating in his book, *Intimacy with God: An introduction to Centering Prayer*, "fear of God" is a technical term in the Old Testament meaning "the right relationship with God." It does not refer to the emotion of fear.

Having a fearless relationship with God is a fundamental understanding that helps develop a deeper relationship with the Divine and the love that is available to you. It is much easier to freely come to God knowing that your relationship is based in love and not fear or judgement. God inflicts no evil punishments onto you, nor does the Divine restrict its love to you. It is we who judge ourselves and restrict ourselves from love.

WILLINGNESS TO LOVE

When you first start to make the choice to love, *you* choose it; however, as you grow in consciousness, you begin to allow for love to choose you. Your willingness to love must come freely, not through a forced effort. We do not forcefully push love onto ourselves or others. Willingness to love means that you become an open vessel for love to flow through you. In your willingness to love, you no longer hold mindsets or practices that drive you away from love. You just remain open and ready to give to what shows up in your life. If you have to force yourself to love, then you are not loving at all. Being an open vessel for love takes you all the way back to the first chapter of this book. You must bypass your mind and just remain open and clear for love to do its work through you.

Ultimately, free will has provided me with my greatest lessons. Through all my ups and downs I have learned that my soul/God has the best laid plans for me. It is my choice to surrender so that I can allow those plans to flow in my life. I have given up the notion that my mind can provide me with accurate directions. I trust in God.

It has been a lifelong battle for me to give up control and to put my trust in God/soul. Many years ago, I got a tattoo on my wrist that said "trust no one." That was my motto when I felt hurt and betrayed. Eventually I decided to have that tattoo changed to say "trust in God". This was a turning point for me. It was a starting point for me to begin to trust God and to eventually learn how to surrender. Trusting the Divine is the start of the right relationship with God. It initiates a friendship. Once you have a friendship with God, you then open the door for a deeper and more intimate relationship to ensue.

TOOLS TO DEEPEN YOUR EXPERIENCE OF THIS CHAPTER

1. Reflect on how you use your free will. Do you follow your mind, or do you look deeper within before you make big life decisions?

2. Ask yourself: What is the will of my soul? Take some time with this question. Ask yourself before your mind takes hold, like before bed or when you first awaken. Then write down your answer. Another tool is to ask before you meditate. During the meditation, let go of

the idea that you will receive an answer. Your answer may just come when you least expect it.

3. Make small steps at surrendering the will of your mind. Notice where and when you can let go of little wants and desires. Work this into your relationships with others, staying present with the moment. Surrender your desire to leave this moment to endlessly chase thoughts in your mind.

4. Take time to work at developing your ability to listen to your heart. Make life an adventure. Spend a day following your inner guidance.

   1. Start by becoming quiet.

   2. Listen and watch for clues. When it feels right or when you get a nudge or a sudden knowingness, act on it.

   3. Do whatever your guidance is telling you. For example, go for a walk. If you are guided, stop into a store. Allow whatever comes. The fun part is to just trust, even if it doesn't make sense to you. The longer you work at being guided, the more interesting it gets.

5. As you keep practicing surrender, bring as much love into your interactions with self and others as you can.

CHAPTER FOURTEEN
AFTER THE AWAKENING

POSITIVE AFFIRMATION: *With a clear and earnest heart and mind, I direct my will to create peace and harmony in my life and in the world.*

After my awakening, my willingness to love began to grow in me. At times I have been more and less aware of my radiance. My awakening was just the beginning. Many things, mainly mindsets and habits, still had to change, and I kicked and screamed while letting go of some of them. Each time I had a new awakening, I shed more of my beliefs and behaviours that no longer seemed to fit. I've had major and minor awakenings, and each time I needed to ground and stabilize the new place in which I found myself.

To fully serve my path and destiny, I have had to include a ruthless, compassionate approach to my devotion and willingness to love myself. The ruthless part involved my sheer willingness to abandon my mind and its trappings, and a steadfast commitment to keep moving forward no matter what comes my way. As for the compassionate part, I needed to become the love that I am.

CHANGE

Several times a year, I would go on meditation retreats with my monk friends. By the end of one of these retreats, I would have a noticeable shift of consciousness and come home a new me. The problem was, I was returning home to the same circumstance that the old me had left.

Then, over a period of several weeks or sometimes only days, the new me would disappear and the old me would resurrect himself like nothing ever happened.

When change happens, it tends to stir up emotions and beliefs, so when you change your mental landscape, there is an adjustment period. Just like your awakenings, some mental shifts are big and some are minor. When you have major mental shifts, it can be very disorienting. I have experienced periods where I felt very confused about everything. Who am I? What does this life really mean? Is this spiritual path I am on just a dream?

Once confusion sets in, my mind is quick to capitalize on it. I begin to have all kinds of distracting thoughts. During these times, I refrain from doing a lot of talking or writing and I try my best to stay anchored to the moment. I remind myself to pay no attention to these thoughts. By doing so, the phase of confusion ends more swiftly.

After an awakening, you experience a phase of integration. If the momentum of your old beliefs runs out before you grab onto them, change takes place. Most often, this wasn't the case for me. I would have a deep experience of awakening and then, the next thing I knew, I was right back into my old beliefs—the very same ones that keep me disempowered and struggling with my life.

The momentum of our old beliefs takes time to burn out. Our old beliefs may have the momentum of our entire life behind them, and it is possible that our beliefs could even have several generations of momentum built into them. It may take all our will power to keep ourselves from grabbing onto our old beliefs. In times of awakening, be extra vigilant not to latch onto your old behaviours or mindsets that keep you from living your new awakening.

THE PATH

Our growth and awakening are not straight lines. Waking up, growing, and letting go has been a whole gamut of experiences for me. There have been times I have had more sideways movement than forward, and it felt like I was going nowhere for long periods. Then, out of the blue, I could see changes in my life, showing me that I no longer struggled with problems that previously caused me stress and pain.

The greatest amount of forward movement has resulted from my willingness to let go of all the behaviours and mindsets that caused me to be disempowered. The energy I would burn up in my grievances was a total waste. My time and energy are much better spent focusing on, and working toward, what is good and in alignment with my purpose.

As I have experienced many difficult periods, I am convinced that we all will have our trials to go through. I have come to see these trials are opportunities to see if we can walk our talk. In difficult situations, the temptation to grab onto the old me jumps right to the front of my mind. It can be just the thing that slides me back into my old, disempowering mindset. Being aware of this helps me stay on track.

The Path of
Awakening and Growth

Growth and awakening is not a straight line by any means. We tend to have just as much sideways movement if not more.

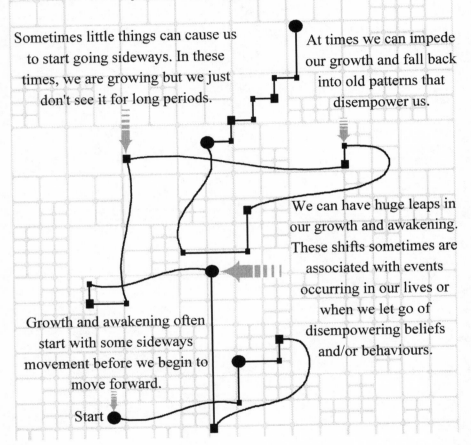

Sometimes little things can cause us to start going sideways. In these times, we are growing but we just don't see it for long periods.

At times we can impede our growth and fall back into old patterns that disempower us.

We can have huge leaps in our growth and awakening. These shifts sometimes are associated with events occurring in our lives or when we let go of disempowering beliefs and/or behaviours.

Growth and awakening often start with some sideways movement before we begin to move forward.

Start

THE PATH DEEPENS WITH LOVE

When we choose for love long enough, eventually everything around us is the result of that choice.

The depth of love in me is immeasurable. For most of my life, I have been drawn to love, and my awakening only intensified a deeper focus toward love. What is different now is that I no longer search for love. I don't require it from another, and I know where to find it in myself. The key point here is that the love I was searching for was always in me.

My life has become a constant reminder to look to love. I have let go of all my beliefs and behaviours that don't support love in my life. This is an ongoing practice that I keep in the forefront of my mind. I no longer want or need anything other than the love I have found in me.

I spent years of my life bouncing between love and my anger. I knew that I needed to let love win, but I had residual anger trapped in me. Years of covered hurt prevented me from being the love that I wanted and needed to be. I found my solution in my choice and willingness to let love in. In turn, this has healed my hurts and has allowed my anger to fade. There are times when it tries to boil up in me, but I am no longer willing to hold my anger. Being my own source of love, I am able to self-regulate. My growth was impeded when I relied on others to give me the love I needed. Becoming my own source of love is my greatest asset. My ability to call up my love within has allowed my growth and further awakening to occur at an exponential rate.

If you like, go back now to the top of this section and replace the word "love" with "God." Notice how this passage deepens when you change the word to God. My relationship with the Divine is about my decision to choose love. It is how I consciously bring God into my life. This is how I stay with God, ceaselessly. Churches, temples, and all the other traditional places of worship are great; however, my relationship with the Divine is completely an inward one that is maintained with me holding a position of love.

GRATITUDE

Since my awakenings, gratitude finds its way into my heart and mind more often. I do not require much and I am grateful for what I have. When my life was void of love/God, my needs were endless. By pausing to reflect on all that I have, gratitude naturally arises in me. When I look back at all the people I have known, and experiences and possessions I have had, I am humbled and filled with gratitude. My gratitude drives away my need for superfluous things now. The pride of ownership holds nothing for me in comparison to the joy of love and peace. It is not that I am opposed to wanting or having things, but the things I want and have do not have the same meaning to me now.

Over time, if we continue to practice gratitude, its wisdom has the power to gift us with the ability to see what really matters in life.

What matters the most to me now is love. The wonderful thing about love is that the more you hold it, the more it gets a hold of you. It also works in reverse. We become what we embrace. The more anger we hold, the more it holds us. The good news is that we can choose what we want to embrace and become that.

KNOWING SELF

After we awaken, there is great joy in shaking off the false self. I discovered that the true self in me has no preferences, wants, or needs. The true self is more than an "object that thinks and wants." My true self holds the plan of my destiny. It is also the same place where I find the Divine radiance within me. The individual sense of self dissolves as I gain a relationship with the true self. As my awakening deepens, the idea that there is a "My" or a "Me" has changed. The identification with the mind and body ties us to the burden of it. We become free the moment we shake off the notion that we are this body.

The body and mind are important, but when it comes to who and what I am, it is much bigger than what is carrying me around. We are merely riding the body we are in. At the end of our life, we will cast it off, and our eternal spirit will be uncovered. Why not unwrap it while we are still in the body and reveal it to the world? We can do this by holding our focus on the identity of the true self and love. The true self is not singular; it is found in all of humanity. I am connected to you as you are connected to me.

By understanding the nature of self, my experience with others and with my life is different. I don't see the world as a dark place riddled with problems that are not mine. I see the world as one massive creation and expression of God. I have my role to play, and most of my attention goes toward that. It is not my job to fix or be anything other than my purpose. Knowing self has turned my life into an interaction to enjoy rather than a struggle to tackle. With love as my purpose, my interaction has become a pursuit of joy. My position of love does not guarantee that I will not experience challenging moments. It just means that I can deal with them from a calm mind, with the intention of love, and with a willingness to look for compassion and understanding.

BEYOND AWAKENING

My awakening was an invitation from the Divine to join God while I transition into my divinity here on earth. It was an invitation to be with God while I go about the rest of my days. What is next is not nearly as important as where I am coming from. What I do does not matter if I am coming from the place of love. What really matters the most to me is the spirit of love. With love, I no longer feel afraid of the future, I no longer feel tormented by my past, and this moment, right now, couldn't be more perfect.

TAKING A TRIP TO A KRISHNA TEMPLE

When I had my retail store in town, a monk from the Krishna temple in Toronto would come and visit me when, once a year, he would ride his bicycle from Toronto to London. We met by chance one year during his annual ride and since that time, every year, it has been the same routine. For many years he would stay for a short visit, and during that visit he would give me his business card and invite me to a Sunday feast. For one reason or another, I could never seem to get myself to the temple to take him up on his invitation. Then one day, while cleaning my desk, I came across one of his cards. I decided in that moment I would go to Toronto on Sunday. I called the temple to let my friend know that I was coming, because I wanted to make sure he was going to be there. I also wanted to know what time first prayers were so I could spend the day with him. When I called, he was elated to get my phone call and confirmed that he would be there and that first prayers were at five.

A few days later, I was on the road at three in the morning to make it to the temple in Toronto by 5:00 a.m. When I arrived, there was a devotee at the front desk. I let him know I was there to visit one of the monks who lived in the temple, and the front desk person said, "I think your friend is still sleeping."

I told him that my friend and I had made arrangements for my visit, so he should be awake, since he did say first prayers were at five. A few minutes later, the receptionist returned with my sleepy-eyed friend stumbling behind him. When they got to the front desk, my friend looked at me and said, "What are you doing here so early?" Instantly it dawned on me. He had meant 5:00 p.m., not 5:00 a.m.

It was an interesting day with my friend. He really didn't know what to do with me. He was not accustomed to having visitors, so all day long he just shuffled me from room to room in the temple. I did not mind that nor did I require a lot of attention from him. It was just nice to be there for the day. What made that day so special, and what makes this story worth telling, is what happened after I met him in the reception area at 5:00 a.m.

Once we figured out that we had a misunderstanding, my friend invited me to sit in the temple while he went off to shower and prepare himself to be my host for the day. From the lobby, I had been able to hear some of the monks chanting Hare Krishna, and I felt drawn to them. As soon as my friend deposited me into the temple, he scurried off to get ready.

Upon entering the room, I was taken aback by its beauty. I was struck speechless from all the statues and shrines of the Hindu Gods to the aroma of incense burning. There were about six monks dancing and singing the Hare Krishna chant, and I was mesmerized by them.

"Hare Krishna, Hare Krishna, Krishna Krishna, Hare Hare
Hare Rama, Hare Rama, Rama Rama, Hare Hare"

I had never heard the Krishna chant sung with such power and devotion. As they sang and danced, I felt like I was in the most beautiful dream and began to experience a high state of bliss.

One of the monks was partially paralyzed. Later I was told that he'd had a stroke. But this did not stop him from dancing and worshiping his lord Krishna. I was so deeply taken by him that I did not even notice the tears of love rolling down my cheeks. I will never forget the pure love and devotion that was pouring out of that monk. Without a word, that monk taught me the true essence of devotion.

By supper time, I was so full of love and devotion I really did not care if I ate or just continued doing meditation. The memory of that day will always be with me.

Devotion to Love

Devotion begets awakening, and awakening begets devotion.

My devotional practice has grown as I have awakened. With my awakening has come an understanding that devotion is the doorway into the deeper states of union with God. The fastest route to our union with the Divine is through love. When we turn our hearts and minds toward loving each other and ourselves, our relationship with God strengthens and grows richer.

I did not become religious or more spiritual. I just became more loving and devoted to staying in the presence of love. This, in turn, has provided me with many great experiences. The relationship I am having with God is based entirely on loving myself and the world around me. It is simple and direct. We do not have to be anything other than who we are.

The simplest and most direct path is to just,

BE LOVE.

SOURCES

Keating, Thomas, *Intimacy with God: An Introduction to Centering Prayer*
The Crossroad Publishing Company, 2017

Keating, Thomas, *A Rising Tide of Silence*
Documentary, 2013
Director: Jones, Peter C.

Hawkins, David R., M.D. Ph.D., *Healing and Recovery*
Veritas Publishing, 2009
The Eye of the I : From Which Nothing is Hidden
Veritas Publishing, 2001
I: Reality and Subjectivity
Veritas Publishing, 2003

Hawkins, David R., M.D. Ph.D., *Letting Go: The Pathway of Surrender*
Hay House, 2012

Goleman, Daniel, *Emotional Intelligence: Why It Can Matter More Than IQ*
Bloomsbury Publishing, 1996

Kornfield, Jack, *After the Ecstasy, the Laundry: How the Heart Grows Wise on the Spiritual Path*
Bantam Books, 2000

Sri Maharaj, Nisargadatta, *I Am That*
The Acorn Press, United States, 1982

Troward, Thomas, *The Edinburgh Lectures on Mental Science*
Dodd, Mead & Company, New York, 1909

Knight, JZ , *Ramtha: The White Book*
JZ. K. Publishing, 1986

Swami Prabhavananda, *Shankara's Crest-Jewel of Discrimination*
Translator: Isherwood, Christopher
Vedanta Press, 1978

Dr. Wolf, Fred Alan, *Double Slit Experiment*
www.fredalanwolf.com or YouTube: "Dr. Quantum Double Slit Experiment."

www.heartmath.org

www. hackernoon.com

McCourt, Malachy
(Resentment quote)
The New York Times **interview, 1998**

Rev. Rose, Safire

Dr. Wattles, Wallace, D, *The Science of Getting Rich*
Elizabeth Towne Publishing. New York, 1910

King James Version of the Holy Bible

Abraham J. Twerski
YouTube, https://www.youtube.com/watch?v=dcUAIpZrwog

Brown, Les, *Live Your Dreams*
(Dog on the Nail story)
William Morrow Paperbacks, 1994

Bhagavad-Gita, *As It Is*
His Divine Grace A. C. Bhaktivedanta Swami Prabhupada
The Bhaktivedanta Book Trust, 1986

Kayyam, Omar, *The Rubaiyat of Omar Kayyam, 1895*
Translation: Fitzgerald, Edward

St. John of the Cross, *The Living Flame of Love*
Translation: E. Allison Peers
Martino Fine Books, 2014

What the Bleep Do We Know!?
Film Producers: Arntz, William, Chasse, Betsy, Vicente, Mark, 2004

Made in the USA
Lexington, KY
07 June 2019